The Yellow Nib

No 9 Summer 2014

Edited by

Leontia Flynn
Frank Ormsby

The Yellow Nib
Edited by Leontia Flynn and Frank Ormsby.

Editorial Board:
Fran Brearton
Edna Longley
Peter McDonald
David Wheatley

Editorial Assistants:
Stephen Connolly
Charlene Small

Printed by:
CDS

Typeset by:
Stephen Connolly

Subscriptions:
Gerry Hellawell
The Seamus Heaney Centre for Poetry
School of English
Queen's University Belfast
Belfast BT7 1NN
Northern Ireland

www.theyellownib.com

Subscription Rates:
£10/€12 per year, for two issues (Great Britain & Ireland)
€20/$25 per year (rest of world)
All subscription rates include postage and packaging.

Back Issues
Numbers 1 – 5, and 8 are available.
£5/€6 per back issue (Great Britain & Ireland)
€10/$15 per back issue (rest of world)
All rates include postage and packaging.

ISBN: 978-1-909131-02-6
ISSN: 1745-9621

Contents

REVIEWS

CIARAN CARSON

FIVE POEMS AFTER FRANCIS PONGE

Cigarette

Let us first set the atmosphere: foggy
yet powder-dry, dishevelled, the cigarette forever
in the thick of what it constantly creates.

Then the personal touch: a pencil-thin torch,
much more fragrant than illuminating, from whose tip
fluffy grey dottles are tapped off in phrases.

Finally, its burning passion: this glowing bud,
shedding itself in a silvery dandruff,
sleeved still in a little muff of recent ash.

CIARAN CARSON

Candle

From time to time the night revives
this extraordinary plant, whose glow rearranges
furnished rooms into great blocks of shadow.

Its golden leaf stands poker-faced
upon a coal-black stalk
perched in the hollow of an alabaster column.

Tatty butterflies bombard it
in lieu of the much too lofty moon
which hazes the woods.

But once singed or frazzled by the fray,
they tremble on the verge of frenzy near to stupor.

Meanwhile the candle, bursting suddenly free
from smoke to flare and flicker on the book,
encourages the reader, whereupon
it tilts over in its dish
to drown in its own juices.

CIARAN CARSON

Vegetation

Rain does not form the only series of hyphens between
the earth and sky: there is another kind, less intermittent,
made of better woven, sterner stuff, which holds its ground
however strong the wind. And if the elements,
according to the season, succeed in breaking off some bits –
endeavouring to pulverise them whirlwind-fashion –
it is evident, when all is said and done, that what
has been dispersed is nothing much to speak of.

Looking more closely into it, we find ourselves at one
of the thousand doors of an immense laboratory,
bristling with omnifarious hydraulic apparatuses
infinitely more intricate than the simple columns
of the rain, so daringly original in concept they
are simultaneously retort and filter, siphon and alembic.

These are the precise instruments the rain
first encounters before it attains the ground.
They receive it in a panoply of little bowls, arranged
in crowds at every level possible, and variously
deep or shallow, overspilling one into the other,
stage by lower stage, until finally the earth is watered.
Thus they slow down the downpour according to
their particular bent, retaining the aqueous humours
and their singular benefit to the soil long after
the passing of the meteorological event.

They alone have the gift to make all types of rain
glitter in the sunlight: in other words, to display,
under the auspices of joy, their font and origin
as religiously acknowledged as they were
precipitately cast by sorrow. Meticulously questing
in their occupation are these enigmatic characters.

They grow in stature in proportion to the rainfall,
but more regularly, and with greater discretion;
and having, as it were, a reservoir of power, they keep on
at it when there is no rain at all. And finally,
moreover, water can be found in certain overblown
ampoules they produce and show off blushingly:
assignations that we call their fruits.

Such, it would seem, are the physical functions
of this tapestry of warp and weft in three dimensions,
on which we have bestowed the name of vegetation
for its other properties, most particularly the kind of life
that animates it ... But I wanted in the first instance
to articulate this point: although their ability
to self-synthesize and to reproduce themselves without
being asked – as seen between the paving stones
of the Sorbonne – connects them somewhat to
the animal realm, that is to say, to every kind
of nomadic species, nevertheless they dwell in certain places
as a permanent fixture, a fabric rooted to the world,
clinging on to it like one of its foundations.

CIARAN CARSON

Oyster

The oyster, the size of a good-sized pebble,
has a more rocky look to it; motley in colour, it is
brilliantly whitish. It is a stubbornly closed world.

Still, one can open it: one must hold it in the hollow
of a tea-towel, then approach it with the stub
of a blunt knife, making several stabs at it.
Exploratory fingers get cut on it, nails broken: filthy work.
Where it's been chipped at, its cover of white tide-marks
bears a serrated halo. The interior reveals

a world of meat and drink beneath
what we can confidently call a 'firmament'
of mother-of-pearl, the skies above sagging into the skies below
to form a single, brackish puddle, a viscid, greenish sachet
that trembles in waves of smell before one's eyes,
its borders fringed with blackish lace.

Sometimes albeit rarely a dental formula
will pearl within its nacre craw,
with which once found you will adorn yourself.

CIARAN CARSON

Mollusc

The mollusc is a being ... almost ... an essence.
It needs no internal scaffolding,
making do with a stronghold,
somewhat like paint in the tube.

In this instance, Madame Nature
scorns to show off plasma in its naked form.
She merely demonstrates how tenderly
she keeps it safe in a trinket-box
whose inner is more fetching than its outer.
No mere gob of mucous spit,
but a reality by far more precious.

The mollusc is endowed with the mighty power
of shutting itself up. In other words it is a clam.

If truth be told it's no more than a muscle,
a hinge – a self-closing hinge at that – and its door,
a self-closing hinge having secreted the door.

Two shallow concave doors
constitute its entire dwelling,
first and last abode.
It lodges there even after death.
Impossible to take it out alive.

The least cell of our body clings as tightly to language
as language has us in its grip.

But sometimes another being comes
to violate the tomb, and, if it deems it fit,
to supplant its late departed builder.

Hence the case of the hermit crab.

ALAN GILLIS

SIX POEMS

The Zeitgeist

I look for you behind retail parks,
ghost-lit showrooms, in dark
scrubland where plastics flutter on coils
of barbed wire; where, through quagged soil
sown with pipes, cartons, slugged condoms,
streams a steep-edged brook. Drawn
to its burble and splurge
I slip on the verge, fall and splunge
stretching for the banks, reeds, not catching hold
of anything sound, my hands ice-cube cold.
And past megastores, waste yards, the suburbs' borders,
carried along on colourless waters
ever gushing on, with no smile, no frown,
I call you down, I call you down.

Ω

City limits are fine, but I spend most
of my time hemmed in and lost
up a tower—in front of a screen,
black plastic keyboard, black plastic machine
on a laminate desk—where the windows
won't open much in case I throw
myself out. Dust gathers on the phone,
empty plant pots. I am alone
much of the time, to the extent
that a vague itch of harassment
prickles my contact with people.
And vacuumed through the non-soul

of blank matter, with no smile, no frown,
I call you down, I call you down.

Ω

Outside on shopped streets swarm mothers,
alpha males, screenagers, old, young, lovers,
the homeless, the bewildered, ill, unique,
the beautiful with their self-as-boutique—
so many, thronged into one body,
surrounding me, squishing, cumbering me
with sucken hair and grey breath,
a cracked open swallowing mouth.
And looking through a million eyes,
slouching upon a million thighs
compelled by the shackles
of meat-headed instinct to slowly circle
around and around, with no smile, no frown,
I call you down, I call you down.

Ω

Inside the machine or, at least, on the screen
I discover everything that has been,
will be, or might never be, has a place.
You can search for God, your name, any face,
and reconfigure. You can hurt someone
and they won't know it was you. There's a room
for all things, the wall of each room an exit
to all that's possible, all interconnected
with, as they say, no edge and no centre.
I press enter and enter and enter
not knowing where to go, what I might find
in this flat expanding surveillant mind,
weightless, free floating, with no smile, no frown,
I commune. Then the machine powers down.

ALAN GILLIS

Instagrammatic

The camera went snap and the moment
was captured. It was a glorious day.
But when I picked up the photograph
weeks later, the image was skew-whiff,
like a cover version of the scene
I remembered. The sky, I'm sure,

was picture-book azure, not pasty duck
egg and mackerel. The trees were Vogue
magazine green but, in our photo, dull
as a self-printed Plymouth Argyle fanzine.
And we were not like ourselves. Life-
sized cardboard cut outs of Mario and Luigi

in a shop window Nintendo display
look more true to life. It was as if look-
alike actors had taken our place
and I imagined a set-up where we pay
stand-ins to replicate scenes of our life
while we work overtime in grey rooms

to pay them. I wondered, what chance
have words, if even in a photograph
from a Sony Cyber-Shot DSC-RX 100
the living moment is caged, held off-stage?
All that we might see or say is half-wrong.
We approximate one another. Then we're gone.

And so, though I've been with you now
for donkey's years, if I were to speak of how
I want to lick your eyebrows, but don't dare risk it,
or say your ears are biscuits,
your teeth scream,
your lips are the crystal violet contours of a recurring dream,

your hair cries,
your nipples are eyes,
your tongue is a lizard,
your passing youth is melting lard
and when you tilt your head at nothing much to surprise me with a grin
I'm a forest of fir trees shoogled in the wind,

and your sense of humour is a ferret,
your nose is a white-sided jackrabbit,
the sweat on the curve of your neck is the dew on a tulip's calyx,
your irises are the aurora borealis
(and if these are windows to your soul, then you're a chameleonic
                                        shimmering megaton
of colliding electric particles blown by the sun),

your stomach is a sand dune,
your dress is a lambent field of wheat blown gently in June,
your legs are identical twins,
your chin is a dove, or, at least, you have a bar of Dove soap for a chin
and when I reach for you I press against a windowpane,
scattered, dripping, splattered drops of shivered rain,

and your heart is an ocean liner that has sunk,
your fingers are a crack team of commandoes, but your toes are drunk,
your laughter is a round of applause,
your bank balance is that scene where Robert Shaw is eaten in Jaws
and I'm sorry I'm a banjaxed replica backstreet device,
all wind and spleen, no fire nor ice,

and your backside is a birthday cake,
your memories are a rainbow cloud of dragonflies above a darkening lake,
your handbag is a pandemonium,
your happiness is summer grass bleaching in the sun
and your remaining days are shorebirds swooping through an almond-streaked
                                        sky over the vast Atlantic's oncoming night,
then remember, my love, I might not be half-right.

ALAN GILLIS

Lunch Break on a Bright Day

If you lie on your back,
buck naked in your clothes,
under a beech or ash
tree's secluded grove

of park grass, letting
time pass with bird
nests above you
and a sound-quilt of bird

song about you,
as if in an alcove
looking up at a sun-spritzed
stained glass window,

watching the city's smoke
billow and waft
in delicate mallow puffs,
creamed meringue rafts

floating in the blue
lagoon sky,
you might come to suspect
the concourse between your eye

and brain,
for just like those old tubed
kaleidoscope toys you put
to your eye and turned

so everything went
Lucy in the Sky,

the sunlight wheels
and turns as you lie

within the umbra
of the tree,
as the rinsing breeze
ripples the leaves

and sashaying twig-tips
with a shush
to the ear,
and each swish

of that green hair sprays the air
with glittered drops of bright
molten flushing amber,
lemon beads of light

in a river of glints,
a gush of glimmer-flow,
so you understand
the proposition *there is no*

fixed position
is now the only
fixed position,
for you can't take in this one tree,

the bark-brown
rutty dark of its bole,
its thick arms
upholding aureoles,

flavescent weavings,
branches sprouting
out of branches,
sprigs and spangs spouting

into a four thousand-
fingered trick of light,
pearl and honey
twinkling through slight

chinks between the leaves,
fast eyes flashed through fronds,
micro-tints of ruby,
wet gleams of blonde

and bottle green,
leaf-tips like the lime
in a sharp tequila
and fizzed lime

soda sparkled with ice
trickling through a thin
multi-leaved
fluent-edged flim

of illuminated green
and aquamarine,
emerald, acid green,
avocado and margarine

until your head dances off,
leaving you with luminance
in a haze of movement,
an overload of sense

and absence of reason
with which to rise
unsteady to your feet,
rub your twizzled eyes

and return to the city's
vast and hurried goad
of information flows,
firewalls, barcodes,

streets that give no pleasure
today when you walk, as you must,
back to work through the rot
and the rust and the ashes and the dust.

ALAN GILLIS

Night Song for Rosie

Look up at the night's wide dome
adrift through the calm of your mind,
an open vat of deep silent wine—

like floating on the lakes of the moon—
reflecting stars, a looking glass of dreams,
your eyes, upon noiseless waters.

These waters will evaporate and rise,
stew and frown into stormy weather
to murk the stars, darken your eyes.

This will come. This will go. Rest your mind,
pressing down, light unto a screen.
Don't let yourself be tormented.

The stars are grapes swelling on a vine,
aching to fall, to be fermented
in the Lake of Softness, Lake of Time.

ALAN GILLIS

No. 8

I'm waiting for a bus.

Ω

There's a man at the bus stop.

Ω

I count the change
in my hand three times
in the space of
twenty-seven seconds.

Ω

The man at the bus stop
does not acknowledge me.

Ω

Neither of us stands still
as if we both need to go
to the toilet.

Ω

I'll go nuts if the bus doesn't

Ω

Ah here it comes, like a big post box.

Ω

I count my change
again and watch to see if the man
will make some sort of signal
to stop the bus
but he's playing it cool
leaving me uncertain
as to whether I should
also play it cool or signal
when the bus indicates to pull
over of its own accord,
which is a relief.

Ω

The driver looks like someone
has just wiped his face
with a monkfish.

Ω

The bus carriage is how I imagine
a train carriage might be
on a night train to Volgograd.
There is a smell of underwear.

Ω

Everyone looks like
they're in an art installation
where the central concept
is they're completely normal.
They don't acknowledge me
with, as it were, studiousness.
I get a seat on my own.

Ω

Yes!

Ω

I wonder if anyone on the bus
is focusing
on a man or on a woman
and is imagining that
that man or woman is thinking
about getting their hole
or about when they last had their hole.

Ω

Then I worry someone might be
wondering the same about me
and I resent the intrusiveness
and begin to wish
I wasn't on the bus
and I read a newspaper
left on the seat next to me
to take my mind off things.

Ω

The bus chugs its way
along the inner city road
a sluggish river
shoals of people on the pavements
all of them looking mad
and beautiful
some touching one another
most not my God
how can it be
this void of substance?

Ω

I mean the newspaper.

Ω

The woman in front
of me has texted
dont spend ur money!!!
really fast

Ω

I should have brought a book,
something with rhythm
and point.
Those priceless devices.
Point and rhythm.
One morning you come down
the stairs and they're gone.
A note on the table.
You recognize them in others,
from time to time,
in the street.

Ω

Busaroo. Busaroo. Bus-a-doodle-doodle-doo.

Ω

Extremely expensive and desirable
large cars of immaculate design
and awesome engineering pass by
like concrete signifiers
of the self-as-sexual-fantasy
of their drivers
who thereby assert their victory
in the perpetual
battle of the body and soul

against the void
while effectively pissing
on the 22000 children
in the world who die
from preventable poverty daily.

Ω

Does one have depths?
To get to them, I'm sure,
one might board a bus.

Ω

There's the man
from the bus stop
getting off the bus
and walking away
his jacket slung
over his shoulder
for it is quite close
walking into the crowd
like he doesn't care
but I think this is to mask
deep cares
as he enters the anonymous
heart of the bruised city
swallowed whole
by the beautiful shoal
of his mad
questing unknown
brothers and sisters.

Ω

Alone and crowded
going in the usual direction
slowly this is the essence

I must acknowledge
of my being.

Ω

A woman has some bother
getting on the bus
not having the right change
saying she didn't know the fare
had changed
as if these days you could not be
aware
that everything changes
except for the principle
that everything changes.

Ω

So much mystery between us
disguised as indifference.

Ω

Such proximity
disguised as distance.

Ω

Aloof and dependent
the antechamber of the soul
could not be solitary and static
although, I'm sure,
it might feel solitary and static.

Ω

We're all in this together.

Ω

The sunlight
as the bus comes
onto North Bridge
gleams glint-bright
scintillating architecture
sometimes I feel like a feather
swept this-a-way lifting
that-a-way through the heavens
of my time and place here
on earth
while nonetheless
sitting on a bus.

ALAN GILLIS

The Gardens

It's four in the morning in East Belfast,
troubled and quiet. I can still see your lips
flame red in the coffin, your clasped
hair bright snazzy white. At least the tulips
of your eyes were shut tight. I turned away
quickly. Like grass in a public park
I felt cropped and trodden. With kids at play
kicking ball, sliding tackles, toeing their turf marks
for goals, you liked the Gardens'
yellers and roses, snoggers and phlox.
Now winter convokes and hardens,
lays siege, blots colours, casts rocks.
To what end, I wonder, six foot
deep and writhing, do new tulips take root?

[POETRY]

BOB COLLINS

A TRIBUTE TO SEAMUS HEANEY

*Bob Collins, Chairman of the Arts Council of Northern Ireland, paid the following
personal tribute at a special event at Belfast's Lyric Theatre celebrating the life
and work of Seamus Heaney (1939-2013):*

When in 1995, I first read Seamus Heaney's Nobel acceptance speech,
'Crediting Poetry', I was transported back more than forty years to the
aerial wire coming through a hole bored in the frame of our kitchen
window by his recollection of listening to the wireless as a child in the
1940s. But I was also dramatically struck by the relevance of his words
to the work I was doing at that time in broadcasting in RTÉ where I
spent thirty years of my life. When he said:

> I had to get close to the actual radio set in order to concentrate my
> hearing and in that intent proximity to the dial I grew familiar with
> the names of foreign stations ... I also got used to hearing the short
> bursts of foreign languages as the dial hand swept round from
> BBC to Radio Éireann, from the intonations of London to those
> of Dublin and even though I did not understand what was being
> said in those first encounters with the gutturals and sibilants of
> European speech, I had already begun a journey into the wideness
> of the world.

With those words, he encapsulated much of the possibility and the
responsibility of broadcasting as a public good, as public service. I
thanked him for it and quoted him often. Perhaps it was that intuitive
understanding that prompted him to give so much of himself to BBC
and to RTÉ. His contributions have enriched the schedules and the
archives of both, for this and, now, for all future generations. But they
were a powerful way for him to play a role as a public person, as a
thinker who posed challenges for all who had ears to hear.

Recalling his own childhood – and by extension all our childhoods –
he spoke of being

schooled for the complexities of his adult predicament, a future where he would have to adjudicate among promptings variously ethical, aesthetical, moral, political, metrical, sceptical, cultural, topical, typical, post-colonial and, taken all together, simply impossible.

Part of his calling, his choice, was to be a source of assistance to all of us in those adjudications. He knew the risks of that public role and expressed them. Writing in 1974, he said that "the idea of poetry as an art is in danger of being overshadowed by a quest for poetry as a diagram of political attitudes." And in his Nobel speech, he spoke of "having to conduct oneself as a poet in a situation of political violence and public expectation. A public expectation, it has to be said, not of poetry as such but of political positions variously approvable by mutually disapproving groups."

For him, it was simple. "The poet", he said, "is on the side of undeceiving the world. It means being vigilant in the public realm."

And he never ceased from lifting deception from the world. He spoke with clarity and rigour. He became a measure, a yardstick, an index of what was good. A moral force. And in the process, he became a spokesman for the entire society, his poetry the voice of the entire community. John Henry Newman said that writers were the "spokesmen and prophets of the human family." Seamus Heaney discharged that duty to the full. In 'From the Republic of Conscience', he challenged "public leaders / ... [to] weep / to atone for their presumption to hold office." Public leaders, mind you, not just political leaders but all who wished to hold public positions. After the ceasefire and before the Belfast Agreement he wrote that "violence was destructive of the trust upon which new possibilities would have to be built." How right and how farsighted he was.

He also said something in *The Government of the Tongue* that we might well reflect on in these times in both jurisdictions on the island when he wrote of poetry that "it does not propose to be instrumental or effective. Instead, in the rift between what's going to happen and what we would wish to happen, poetry holds attention for a space, functions not as a distraction, but as pure concentration, a focus where our power of concentration is concentrated back on ourselves." It has resonance for our consideration of all the arts.

Last night there was a clip of an interview with Seamus in an RTÉ bulletin. In it he said "If poetry and the arts do anything they can fortify your inner life - your inwardness. Listening together and knowing things together – which is what a culture is. If you know things together that you value, that is a kind of immunity system against things." This wisdom in an interview conducted quickly on the fringes of a public event.

It is difficult to put into words and to convey fully how intimately his person and his poetry had become bound up with the life of the people, especially, I think, and in my experience, in the Republic. How deeply he had become embedded in the affection of the people and in the life of the society - as no artist I can think of has ever quite achieved before. He had an extraordinary place in the public realm.

But that place in the public realm, his presence at state and solemn occasions was not as a symbol of state or as part of state but as a reminder to state of the importance of values, of the challenge of office, of the meaning of society, of the responsibility of leadership to the people, of the place of conscience. Through his life and through his poetry he spoke to the people. And the people listened.

He was intuitively trusted; his integrity appreciated; his directness reciprocated; his dignity sublime.

Two weeks ago, last night, I was in Lisdoonvarna, at the Merriman summer school at which he and Michael Longley gave a public reading. It was an unbelievable experience, powerfully moving and indelibly impressive. The intimacy of the relationship with the capacity audience and their appreciation of the work of both poets will remain forever in the memory. These were two poets who had done much to give poetry back to the people. This was Seamus Heaney being the voice of the community within the community.

I had the particular pleasure of being next to them both at dinner before the reading and, with our spouses - Marie, Edna and Mary, in the small bar of Sheedy's hotel afterwards for nightcap, story, reflection, friendship and fun. It was a delight. More than that, it was a blessing.

Like his life, a blessing whose cup of bounty will flow all the days of our lives.

31/08/13

FRED JOHNSTON

THREE POEMS

The Nakedness of Trees

He was troubled by the nakedness of trees
In winter, the sky like an unwashed plate
The savagery of suicides and the rage of time
The muscular slipperiness of sex
All that effort and the embarrassment
That is a man pulling on his trousers in the dark.

But there were compensations –
When he drove at night up highways whipped
Under the S&M of slick headlights he saw
Towns pulling themselves together through
Fat mists, bright as hallucinations, distant
As dreams, towns that did and did not exist.

Intrusive beauty, naked as trees in winter
Made him think of paintings he'd seen
And passages from books came to him
Even as the road signs lied and sniggered
He considered Chekov, and a degenerate
Macula made a Bacon out of his woman's face.

A man pulling on his trousers in the dark
Is a tree pulling on its leaves
The woman in the sheets is snow falling
Without a sound, piling in the dark and settling
Deep and cold and content; driving at night
He feels her scent settle too on the steering wheel.

FRED JOHNSTON

Big Bang Theory

The young call a man of thirty old
they get born with the Big Bang, the beginning
of time
nothing before it but a rattling of spoons in the dark
guitarists who really played guitars
the boring black sky, godless nebulae, dead stars

who did stupid things like crash cars
or have heart-attacks on toilets
burger-hearted
or get shot by lost boys in front of New York hotels
a miasma of lizard kings
banned novels, all unreadable, all printed on paper

how dull and endless, endless and dull
riots, barricades, a bogside priest with a hankie
a naked girl
on fire far away, a photo of a girl, not a real girl
the word celeb was lacking
there was nothing at all to do, so why did people

not commit suicide and be done with it, like now
why hold on, or hold out, or merely hold
like bats
in a cave
upside-down
to slender grippings in the roof of the cosmos –

theories and spectacles and napalm
and the Fall of The Wall and the rest of it
dead sharks
in a tank, call it Art, an unmade bed, Art again
how dull and pitiless, pitiless and dull
a rattling of spoons in the dark; so, like, *fucked*?

FRED JOHNSTON

Bomb

Weather's drawing its nails down the door
the paintwork looks like savaged skin
a gasp of sour milk reeks at the open fridge door
the garden's gone for the jungular
chimes drip on bare branches like frozen tears
there hasn't been a sod turned in years

how did the house grow grass in the gutters
the walls yellow with nicotine
blown seeds like a pox clotted the gutters
there was no will for appearances
when the place began to lose its will to live
there wasn't even a toss left to give –

there's a ticking in the walls at odd hours
as if the house were a watch or a bomb
patient and timed, counting down the hours
a switch in its heart waiting to trip
the houses, the trees, every spar and door
will shout some salutation and disappear.

EVA BOURKE
translates JAN WAGNER

THREE POEMS

the mission

one good friday father fernando ended up
in a casserole
and father sebastiano's legs swelled
so colossally

he seemed to be sitting on flour sacks.
father juan
finally, who vanished one day singing
in the rain

forest. as for me: I grow my roses, ring
the cool bell that
hangs in the tower like a drop
inside a throat,

study books to which the mould adds
whole appendices,
while an ara breaks loose from the undergrowth
and with a cough takes

wing. the children, their nameless fruit
and red wreaths
of chocho seeds. at night in my room
the wraith

of a mosquito net carries me through the dark
inside its pale
belly; my lamp's the flicker of
an electric eel

in a stream. no sound when I appear in the village
clad in the shadow
of my soutane. nothing stirs. in the morning
I thought I smelled snow.

EVA BOURKE
translates JAN WAGNER

maize

it is a field in which you get lost
while playing, when the shadow falls
longer, and hectare or verst
of field, of wind, of field

separate you from home.
rustle of leaves – like playing cards
being shuffled. later among masses of stars
a new constellation: the zigzagging hare.

you sleep, curled up like an animal.
it is morning when the sun finds
you with your skull

split by thirst. above you these
meters-high swaying shapes, mouths
grinning full of golden teeth.

EVA BOURKE
translates JAN WAGNER

elegy for knievel

„ God take care of me – here I come … "

the landscape grew blurred as soon as it saw him
a daredevil, a hell of a guy,
with a shirt full of stars
and always pursued by the hornet swarm
of engine noise. bones broke,
bones knitted again, and he jumped.

how many obstacles between ramp
and that distant point?
how many disused double-deckers?
did any doubt ever gnaw
inside him till an entire canyon gaped
with sand trickling from the edges,
the screams of large birds?

afternoons when history
stilled for a moment
to scents of popcorn and exhaust.
like here, in yakima, washington,
with this battered moon above the stadium
and thousands catching their breath:
fifteen, twenty buses and the wheel
high in the air.

FRAN BREARTON

THOMAS HARDY AND IRISH POETRY

Where I mean to be
For all that, this New Year's Eve
Is Hardy country,
Lychgate and hoarfrost country,
In search of a darkling thrush.
      – Seamus Heaney, 'Linked Verses'[1]

I.

In his 1929 war memoir *Goodbye to All That*, Robert Graves offers a pen-portrait of Thomas Hardy, based on a visit he made, with his wife Nancy Nicholson, to Hardy's Dorchester home, Max Gate, in the summer of 1920. The sketch is affectionately drawn, but Graves is not above serving his own ends too:

I wrote out a record of the conversation we had with him. He welcomed us as representatives of the post-war generation. He said that he lived such a quiet life in Dorchester that he feared he was altogether behind the times. He wanted, for instance, to know whether we had any sympathy with the Bolshevik regime, and whether he could trust the *Morning Post*'s account of the Red Terror. [...] He asked whether I wrote easily, and I said that this poem was in its sixth draft and would probably be finished in two more. 'Why!', he said, 'I have never in my life taken more than three, or perhaps four, drafts for a poem. I am afraid of it losing its freshness.' [...] He talked of early literary influences, and said that he had none at all, for he did not come of literary stock. [...] (His taste in literature was certainly most unexpected. Once when Lawrence had ventured to say something disparaging against Homer's *Iliad*, he protested: 'Oh, but I admire the *Iliad* greatly. Why, it's in the *Marmion* class!'...) [...] In his opinion *vers libre*

---

1 Published in the *Irish Times*, 30 December 2000. The poem was later shortened and rewritten to become 'Midnight Anvil' in *District and Circle* (2006).

could come to nothing in England. 'All we can do is to write on the old themes in the new styles, but try to do a little better than those who went before us.'[2]
The sting is in the parenthetical tail of this passage, which incidentally is patronising towards Walter Scott as well as Hardy: this is classic and classical public school/Oxbridge snobbery towards what is 'other' at its worst. Also implicit here is the knowingness of the Great War survivor, attuned to the modern political zeitgeist, set against the uncomprehending older generation, who still read the newspapers with some degree of trust. That generation is treated in *Goodbye to All That* with some hostility, and newspaper reportage is subjected to ironic scrutiny: Hardy's question about the *Morning Post* shows a more benign humour at work, but it is still mockery for all that. The representation of Hardy here is one of the reasons Sassoon and Graves fought so bitterly in the aftermath of the publication of *Goodbye to All That*. Sassoon complained to Graves in 1930 that 'There was too much about you and too little about [Hardy's] greatness. The picture of him in your book is misleading, because it shows his simplicity without his impressiveness. Also you have got the *Marmion* anecdote wrong. I was there when it happened'. Graves responded with characteristic arrogance: 'I admired Hardy as a good, consistent, truthful man; I do not believe in *great* men. I treat everyone as an equal unless they prove themselves inferior'. One might have much sympathy therefore with Sassoon's last letter on the subject to Graves (a letter which effectively marks the end of their friendship) when he writes 'I wish you'd broken your rule, for once, and regarded T.H. as your superior until you found that you were his equal.'[3]

It's easy to dismiss this as mere squabbling, a kind of squabbling that Hardy's writing and reputation transcend. But there is a thread here pulled by other writers and critics in ways which have affected – and continue to affect – understanding of Hardy's profile and influence, both in the English tradition, and in the critically more neglected archipelagic context, notably in Ireland. As Donald Davie

---

2 Robert Graves, *Good-bye to All That* (London: Jonathan Cape, 1929), 374-5, 376, 378-9.
3 SS to RG, 7 Feb 1920; RG to SS, 20 Feb. 1920; SS to RG, 2 Mar. 1920. In *Broken Images: Selected Letters of Robert Graves* 1914-1946, ed. Paul O'Prey (London; Hutchinson, 1982), 198, 201, 204.

once observed, 'affection' for Hardy the poet is often 'ruinously shot through with protectiveness, even condescension. Hardy is not thought of as an intellectual force.'[4] Graves's pen-portrait of Hardy, the very fact of his recording the conversation, might be interpreted as literary adulation, but it reads rather more as anthropological curiosity – Hardy as the strange unworldly creature sprung illiterate and Antaeus-like from the soil. 'Good', 'consistent', 'truthful' are admirable qualities: but one might as well add 'mediocre', 'uncritical' (in the pejorative sense of not knowing 'good' literature from 'bad'), naïve, and have done.

Three years later, in his influential study *New Bearings in English Poetry* (1932), F.R. Leavis draws on Graves's memoir to reinforce his own judgement on Hardy:

Hardy is a naïve poet of simple attitudes and outlook. [...] He was betrayed into no heroic postures. He felt deeply and consistently, he knew what he felt and, in his best poems, communicated it perfectly. But there was little in his technique that could be taken up by younger poets, and developed in the solution of their own problems. His originality was not of the kind that goes with a high degree of critical awareness: it went, indeed, with a naïve conservatism. 'In his opinion', reports Mr Robert Graves in his superb autobiography, *Goodbye to All That*, '*vers libre* could come to nothing in England...' [...] The main impulse behind his verse is too commonly the mere impulse to write verse: 'Any little old song, will do', as he says. And, often to the lilt of popular airs, with a gaucherie compounded of the literary, the colloquial, the baldly prosaic, the conventionally poetical, the pedantic, and the rustic, he industriously turns out his despondent anecdotes, his 'life's little ironies', and his meditations upon a deterministic universe and the cruel accident of sentience. [...] That the setting, explicit or implied, is generally rural is a point of critical significance. Hardy was a countryman, and his brooding mind stayed itself habitually upon the simple pieties, the quiet rhythms, and the immemorial ritual of rustic life.

It is very largely in terms of the absence of these, or of any

---

4 Donald Davie, *Thomas Hardy and British Poetry* (London: Routledge & Kegan Paul, 1973), 5.

equivalent, that the environment of the modern poet must be described.[5]

New Bearings famously advocates Eliot's aesthetic in opposition to what Leavis sees as the defunct modes of Hardy, or of Georgian verse: Hopkins is rescued from the nineteenth century, and 'felt to be a contemporary';[6] but the real drive of the book is to argue that Eliot's is the 'strong originality' that 'triumph[s] over traditional habits', that 'in his work by 1920 English poetry had made a new start'.[7] Leavis also comes to this bold conclusion: 'It does not seem likely that it will ever again be possible for a distinguished mind to be formed...on the rhythms, sanctioned by nature and time, of rural culture.'[8]

As Edna Longley observes, 'in Leavis's version of emergent modern poetry, Eliot has out-manoeuvred Yeats', and in *New Bearings* we can also 'glimpse the hegemonic advance of T.S. Eliot's critical dicta'.[9] Eliot's consistent negativity towards Hardy is of relevance here too. In *After Strange Gods*, Eliot berates Hardy for his lack of either 'institutional attachment' (the Church) or 'objective beliefs'. 'He seems to me', Eliot goes on, 'to have written as nearly for the sake of "self-expression" as a man well can; and the self which he had to express does not strike me as a particularly wholesome or edifying matter of communication. He was indifferent even to the prescripts of good writing: he sometimes wrote overpoweringly well, but always very carelessly'.[10] Hardy's novels have 'a note of falsity', stemming from his 'deliberately relieving some emotion of his own at the expense of the reader'.[11] As poet, he fares little better at Eliot's hands. In a *Criterion* editorial coinciding with Yeats's 70th birthday, Eliot observes that Yeats's 'influence upon English poetry has been great and beneficial; upon Irish poetry it seems to me to have been disastrous. And...this is just what you should expect. For a great English poet to have a great

---

5 F.R. Leavis, *New Bearings in English Poetry* (1932; London: Penguin, 1963), 47-8, 49-50.

6 Ibid. 142.

7 Ibid. 62, 70

8 Ibid. 71-2.

9 Edna Longley, *Yeats and Modern Poetry* (New York: Cambridge UP, 2013), 149.

10 T.S. Eliot, *After Strange Gods: A Primer of Modern Heresy* (London: Faber, 1934), 54.

11 Ibid. 56.

influence in England, he must be considerably removed in time: for a literature can be fertilised by its own earlier periods as well as by contemporaries from outside'. If this already negates any possible Hardy-influence on English poetry, the point is then made explicit in the following comparison: 'Of the absolute greatness of any writer, men living in the same period can make only a crude guess. But it should be apparent at least that Mr. Yeats has been and is the greatest poet of his time. Thomas Hardy, who for a few years had all the cry, appears now, what he always was, a minor poet.'[12]

II.

Leavis couldn't predict the future – witness his investment in Ronald Bottrall over W.H. Auden – though like all canon-makers he tried. (His conclusions relating to poetry and rural culture, for instance, are more questionable in the Irish tradition – of which more anon; similarly, Eliot's views on Yeats and English poetry leave open, if inadvertently, the reverse possibility – Hardy's beneficial influence on Irish poetry.) Yet at the time, and in the decades following the publication of *New Bearings*, both Leavis's arguments, and Eliot's habitual hostility towards Hardy's work were sufficiently influential to affect, adversely, Hardy's critical standing. They were also sufficiently extreme to help prompt the anti-modernist backlash in England of the 1950s – a backlash which itself has a knock-on effect on Hardy's reputation. If after death, the poet, as Auden famously said in his elegy for Yeats, '[becomes] his admirers', then Hardy's admirer Larkin has also conditioned critical perceptions of his precursor – and not perhaps entirely in the way he intended. It is a critical commonplace to say that Larkin, between his first and second collections, *The North Ship* in 1945 and *The Less Deceived* in 1955, 'found' his own voice by exchanging Yeats's influence for Hardy's. 'I spent', he writes in 1965, 'three years trying to write like Yeats, not because I liked his personality or understood his ideas but out of infatuation with his music...[I]t is a particularly potent music...and has ruined many a better talent. [...] Every night after supper before opening my large dark green manuscript book I used to limber up by turning the pages of the 1933 plum-coloured Macmillan edition.... When reaction came

12 T.S. Eliot, 'Editorial', *The Criterion* vol. XIV no. LVII (July 1935), 612.

[through reading Hardy's poems], it was undramatic, complete and permanent.'[13] Hardy's distance from a metropolitan 'centre' appeals to a poet who writes of his own 'need to be on the periphery of things'. What he also learns from Hardy is, he says in 1982, 'not to be afraid of the obvious'.[14]

Larkin takes some of the terms by which Leavis critiques Hardy, and makes of them a case for a rather different 'bearing' in English poetry. Asked for his views on poetry in 1955, he produced the following (now notorious) statement: 'As a guiding principle I believe that every poem must be its own sole freshly created universe, and therefore have no belief in "tradition" or a common myth-kitty or casual allusions in poems to other poems or poets...'[15] Leavis on the other hand, even if sometimes and misleadingly associated with the New Criticism, did not believe the poem was its own self-contained universe; he is the great advocate of the great tradition; and allusiveness is at the heart of Eliot's 1920s enterprise. Dismissal here of the 'common myth-kitty' (contra Eliot's endorsement of the 'mythical method' in Yeats and Joyce) is also a dismissal of a Yeatsian 'anima mundi', that 'storehouse' of symbols, or of Yeats's later 'Vision'. Hardy may be read as conscripted by Larkin – the Larkin who professed, however misleadingly, to spurn what is 'foreign' – on national grounds too, against the Irish and American ('international') voices of Yeats, Joyce, Eliot and Pound. What is 'other' is rejected in the interests of navel-gazing at a microcosmic England: whether that 'England' finds its centre in Dorchester or Hull really doesn't matter, as long as it's not Berlin, Dublin, Paris – or even London.

So Larkin 'rescues' Hardy from Eliot and Leavis for a new generation. But he does so in oppositional terms that don't accurately reflect Hardy's relation to poets such as Yeats, or indeed reflect the complex play of influences in Larkin's own aesthetic. It is as much a critical commonplace now to point out that Yeats's influence persists in Larkin's work. Hardy and Yeats, rather than one displacing the other,

13 Philip Larkin, *Required Writing: Miscellaneous Pieces 1955-1982* (London: Faber, 1983) 29.
14 Ibid. 55, 67.
15 Ibid. 79.

represent twin poles of Larkin's aesthetic, complementary figures onto whom he projects different aspects of a divided self. But this is not how Larkin chose to view the matter in the Hardy affirmations found so habitually in his critical writings from the 1950s to the early 1980s, and the existence of this kind of Yeats-Hardy opposition is, on the whole, also how Donald Davie reads the situation in the early 1970s. In *Thomas Hardy and British Poetry* (1973) Davie sets out the powerful thesis that 'in British poetry of the last fifty years (as not in American) the most far-reaching influence, for good and ill, has been not Yeats, still less Eliot or Pound, not Lawrence, but *Hardy*'. It is an influence, he concedes, that not all poets are prepared to acknowledge, notably in the case of Irish, Scottish and Welsh poets 'who do not care to be indebted to such an intransigently English poet as Hardy'. Yet while Davie, by contrast, rightly points towards Hardy's influence on Austin Clarke and others, he also argues that Hardy 'has the effect of locking any poet whom he influences into the world of historical contingency, a world of specific places at specific times',[16] with the consequence that:

> Hardy appears to have mistrusted, and certainly leads other poets to mistrust, the claims of poetry to transcend the linear unrolling of recorded time. This is at once Hardy's strength and his limitation; and it sets him irreconcilably at odds with for instance Yeats, who exerts himself repeatedly to transcend historical time by seeing it as cyclical, so as to leap above it into a realm that is visionary, mythological, and (in some sense or to some degree) eternal. It ought to be possible for any reader to admire and delight in both Hardy and Yeats, if only because so much of the finest Yeats is concerned with the effort of transcendence rather than the achievement of it. But for any poet who finds himself in the position of choosing between these two masters, the choice cannot be fudged; there is no room for compromise.[17]

As for Yeats himself on the subject of Hardy – whom he met in 1912, dining with Henry Newbolt at Max Gate and presenting Hardy with a Royal Society of Literature gold medal – his occasional comments are not encouraging, even if he did, along with 42 other poets, contribute

---

16 Davie, *Thomas Hardy and British Poetry*, 3-4.

17 Ibid. 4.

a handwritten poem in 1919 to mark Hardy's 79th birthday.[18] Yeats read Lionel Johnson's *The Art of Thomas Hardy* in 1894 (a study of the fiction; Hardy's first volume of poems did not appear until 1898) and observed: 'I feel...that there is something wrong about praising Hardy in a style so much better than his own. I wish [Lionel] had written instead of Dante or Milton'.[19] As Louis MacNeice notes, when it comes to the poetry, Yeats 'conveniently' forgot about Hardy and Housman when it suited him[20] – more particularly, one might add, when he wished to identify the trends and failings of modern poetry and associate those trends with England rather than Ireland. Yeats's argument that Irish poetry 'moves in a different direction and belongs to a different story'[21] is a necessary distancing of himself from Eliot and modernism. In Yeats's introduction to the 1936 *Oxford Book of Modern Verse*, if Hardy does come off better than Eliot (who, according to Yeats, 'produced his great effect...because he has described men and women that get out of bed or into it from mere habit'), the brief mention of Hardy is a less than ringing endorsement, and his achievement compares unfavourably to Synge's:

In Ireland, [there] still lives almost undisturbed the last folk tradition of western Europe...but the reaction from rhetoric, from all that was prepense and artificial, has forced upon...writers now and again, as upon my own early work, a facile charm, a too soft simplicity. In England came like temptations. *The Shropshire Lad* is worthy of its fame, but a mile further and all had been marsh. Thomas Hardy, though his work lacked technical accomplishment, made the necessary correction through his mastery of the impersonal objective scene. John Synge brought back masculinity to Irish verse with his harsh disillusionment...[22]

---

18 See Ralph Pite, *Thomas Hardy: The Guarded Life* (London: Picador, 2006), 441.

19 W.B. Yeats to Olivia Shakespear, 6 August 1894, *The Letters of W.B. Yeats*, ed. Allan Wade (London: Rupert Hart-Davis, 1954), 235

20 Louis MacNeice, *The Poetry of W.B. Yeats* (1941; London: Faber, 1962), 87.

21 W.B. Yeats, 'Modern Poetry: A Broadcast', *Essays and Introductions* (Dublin: Gill and Macmillan, 1961), 506-7.

22 W.B. Yeats, 'Introduction', *The Oxford Book of Modern Verse* (Oxford: Clarendon Press, 1936), p.xiii., xxi

III.

If all this might seem to reinforce Davie's argument for irreconcilable differences between Yeats and Hardy, Davie's contemporary, Denis Donoghue, has painted a different picture (Davie and Donoghue were based, respectively, at TCD and UCD in the 1950s). Contributing to 'A Yeats Symposium' for the *Guardian* in 1989, marking the fiftieth anniversary of Yeats's death, Donoghue observes that:

> Increasingly, it seems unsatisfactory to think of Yeats in relation to Modernism; or, to be precise, in close association with Pound and Eliot. [...] Released from these affiliations, Yeats now seems a major poet within the large context of post-romantic poetry; he is closer to Hardy and Stevens than to Eliot, Pound, Joyce, or Wyndham Lewis. [...] He seems to be a poet comparable to Hardy for accomplishment and scale; like Hardy a great poet of love and death and the other perennial themes.[23]

Donoghue's phrasing is ('seems') tentative, but to associate Yeats most closely, not with international modernism, but with a poet once seen as the quintessence of a provincial Englishness, marks a sea-change. And that sea-change probably owes something to the work of Irish poets who, from the 1970s-1980s onwards, have asserted Hardy's relevance to modern Irish poetry.

In that context, we might recall the review by A.N. Wilson in the *Spectator* in 1982 of Motion and Morrison's *The Penguin Book of Contemporary British Poetry*:

> Yeats, Hugh MacDiarmid and Dylan Thomas all wrote English poetry. British poetry sounds about as appetising as Traveller's Fare on British Rail. This *British* business was started by the BBC when they began to flood the air with programmes and voices from Northern Ireland. [...] Seamus Heaney is...described solemnly as 'the most important new poet of the last 15 years, and the one we very deliberately put first in our anthology'. 'Important' is the give-away word here. No one can seriously pretend that Heaney is a particularly good or interesting poet. He certainly is not in the same class as Yeats, with whom he has been compared. He is not half as good as Geoffrey Hill or Ted Hughes. Yet for some reason he was

---

23 'A Yeats Symposium', *Guardian*, 27 Jan. 1989, 25-6.

taken up by the Sunday-newspaper dons...since when his quietly
minor accomplishments have been smothered in self-importance,
his own and that of his admirers. If Heaney is 'major', what word do
you use to describe Wordsworth? At his best, Heaney writes sub-
Paterian prose-poems, with the rural life of Ulster as his theme.
But...Heaney has nothing whatever to *say*.[24]
A.N. Wilson on Heaney in 1982, in one of the worst instances of
getting it wrong, is rather reminiscent, in its essentials, of F.R. Leavis
on Hardy in 1932 (although Wilson's deliberately provocative mud-
slinging here is a far cry from Leavis's considered scholarship). Both
Hardy and Heaney are minor poets of minor accomplishments, with
rural life as a theme ('provincial' isn't said, but it's there), meaning
in effect, they have 'nothing' to say to today's world. It strikes some
chords too with Eliot's observation that Hardy had 'all the cry', that
his reputation had been over-inflated.

When Leavis observed that there was 'little in [Hardy's] technique
that could be taken up by younger poets and developed in the solution
of their own problems' he may have had a partial point, in as much as
it is Hardy's subject-matter and aesthetic positioning more than his
technique that influence the Irish poetic tradition. Yet what Leavis
could not foresee was the emergence of a cultural context in Northern
Ireland that posed particular problems for poets – the violent collision
of tradition and modernity; the elegist's need to speak out and yet
the guilt in doing so; the redefinition of the supposed periphery as
an aesthetic (and in Northern Ireland political) centre; the need to
reinvent and yet retain traditional forms – in the addressing of which
Hardy could serve as exemplar. Nor could Leavis foresee that it would
once more be possible once again for a reputation and a mind to be
formed 'on the rhythms...of rural culture'.

The terms by which Leavis dismisses Hardy as a negligible influence
– a 'countryman' writing about 'rustic life' with a supposedly 'naïve'
formal conservatism and an 'outsider' status – are the ones which now
seem to confirm his importance. (Not least, the ecocritical debates of
recent years serve to reorient thematic priorities.) The rural, the local,
the manipulation of traditional rhythms – these are all the things

---

24 A.N.Wilson, 'A Bloodless Miss', *Spectator*, 27 November 1982, 28-9.

that give Heaney the 'international' purchase which for Leavis would have been, ironically, one of the measures of greatness. It's Leavis's 'metropolitan' stance and his association of *vers libre* with originality that now look rather dated, not Hardy. And Leavis also overlooks the area where Hardy helps to redefine a genre for his inheritors, which is as elegist. As Jahan Ramazani argues, in his study of modern elegy from Hardy to Heaney, Hardy 'reinvigorates the elegy by helping to shift its psychic bases from the rationalizing consolations of normative grief to the more intense self-criticisms and vexations of melancholic mourning'.[25] Where Yeats links his mourning work to 'a disappearing aristocratic vision', Hardy 'associates his...with a threatened rural outlook'[26]: in that sense he is an important influence for a contemporary generation, repelled by Yeats's autocratic politics if not by his forms. Ramazani argues convincingly that Hardy's elegies anticipate those of Yeats, Eliot and Pound, that he is a 'key transitional figure' who 'presages the tension in much 20th century poetry between the elegiac and the anti-elegiac'.[27] The intensities of the Northern Irish experience over the last four decades, a site of contested memory and space, with its tensions between religious tradition and secularity, have brought elegy into particular focus. The Great War protest-elegy offers one model for Northern Irish poets; and behind it is Hardy's *Poems of 1912-13*. (One of the poems A.N. Wilson derides – Heaney's 'Casualty' – is in an obvious rhythmical dialogue with Yeats, more particularly with Yeats's 'The Fisherman'; but its speaker's guilt in the mourning process also owes something to Hardy, as do its rhythms of rural life.)

Radical in terms of genre, Hardy is also 'both conservative and radical in matters of form': he 'adheres to the metered line but roughs up prosodic and syntactic polish; he appropriates Romantic diction but fashions many jarring locutions'.[28] There are echoes here of J.M. Synge's expressed need for verse to be 'brutal', or later of Heaney's desire to 'take the English lyric and make it eat stuff that it has never

---

25 Jahan Ramazani, *Poetry of Mourning: The Modern Elegy from Hardy to Heaney* (Chicago and London: University of Chicago Press, 1994), 5.

26 Ibid. 13.

27 Ibid. 34.

28 Ibid. 36.

eaten before'.[29] Like Hardy, Northern Irish poets have come under fire for their adherence to traditional forms and yet have always rejected a too-easy association of experimental form with anti-hierarchical politics. And, not least, Hardy as the poet of place plays an important role in the aesthetic development of Heaney, Longley, or Paulin.

If critics have perhaps been slow to pick up on Hardy's presence in the contemporary Irish poetry scene (a notable exception is Tara Christie's article, 'Seamus Heaney's Hardy' from 2004), this is not necessarily true of the poets themselves. Tom Paulin's first critical book is *Thomas Hardy: The Poetry of Perception* (1975), based on his graduate thesis. It bears the marks of his friendship with (and mentoring by) Douglas Dunn, both of whom studied at Hull, overlapping with Larkin's time as librarian there. In the introduction to the book, Paulin's concern is, in part, to differentiate his work from, and quarrel with, Davie's 1973 *Thomas Hardy and British Poetry*. Davie comes under fire for insufficient appreciation of Douglas Dunn's work, and for anxieties that aren't Hardy's problem but Davie's (what Paulin detects as his 'dissatisfaction with a confused entity composed of Hardy's poetry, English suburban sprawl, and certain British poets').[30] He also rescues Hardy and Larkin from Davie's critique of their limited horizons, and in doing so (as elsewhere in the book) opts for comparison with Yeats on some fundamental principles, in spite of their obvious differences:

> When Davie criticizes Hardy and Larkin for infrequently breaking into, 'without meaning to and without noticing', imaginative levels that Tomlinson continually inhabits, we ought to be aware of just how thin the air up there can be. Yeats, who is Hardy's opposite, knew this.[31]

Paulin's study also comes at a time when he was working on his first collection, *A State of Justice*, published in 1977, poems whose tone, idiom, and forms are familiar enough to those who know Dunn's early poetry, or Larkin's work. 'Inishkeel Parish Church' evidences the debt to both:

> Standing at the gate before the service started,

---

29 Quoted in Neil Corcoran, *Poets of Modern Ireland* (Cardiff: University of Wales Press, 1999), 177.

30 Tom Paulin, *Thomas Hardy: The Poetry of Perception* (London: Macmillan, 1975), 6.

31 Ibid. 10.

In their Sunday suits, the Barrets talked together,
Smiled shyly at the visitors who packed the church
In summer...
[...]
Then, before the recognitions and the talk,
There was an enormous sight of the sea,
A silent water beyond society.

In 1986, *Thomas Hardy: The Poetry of Perception* was published in a second edition, with a new introduction. This time Paulin begins, not with Grigson, but by ecumenically associating Hardy with Hopkins, and the positioning of the work on Hardy has completely changed. Paulin is no longer tinkering around the edges of Donald Davie and British poetry; this is a new 'funky' Hardy for Ireland in the 1980s, and for a 'new' Tom Paulin. Both Hopkins and Hardy, he argues, 'hold to an aesthetic of "cunning irregularity" and aim for a poetry of syncopated texture rather than melodious veneer. For them, the highest form of poetic language is rapid, extempore, jazz-like and "funky".'[32] Both are associated with a Gothic tradition. That tradition 'is northern and consonantal and its roots are in the people rather than in the court. The Gothic poet writes poems that have a fricative, spiky, spoken texture... [with a] populist delight in rough, scratchy sounds...'. Through such writers, he argues, 'literary English has been periodically refreshed by an Antaeus-like contact with the earth'.[33] Furthermore, Hardy (like Paulin himself?) is, in this reading, anti-(British) establishment:

Imperialist, racist, reactionary, sexist...Tennyson is in brilliant command of a dead language. [...] Hardy belongs outside this institutional, official reality. He grew up in a rural society where most people spoke dialect and where illiteracy was normal. [...] As a writer, Hardy was caught between a provincial oral culture of song, talk, legend, and a metropolitan culture of print, political power and what linguists used to term R.P....And when Hardy asserted that a "certain provincialism of feeling" was invaluable in a writer and set that idea against Arnold's idea of culture – an idea hostile to provincialism – he was referring to a mode of feeling that is bound

---

32 Tom Paulin, *Thomas Hardy: The Poetry of Perception* (2nd ed. London: Macmillan, 1986), 3.

33 Ibid. 3-4.

in with song, dialect, physical touch, natural human kindness and what he terms "crude enthusiasm". He does not mean provincial in the Chekhovian sense of stifled ambition and anxious mediocrity. Partly the revision of the introduction here brings it into line with Paulin's changed political thinking in the 1980s, as a (protestant) republican concerned with the 'Language Question' in Ireland, about the politics of Ulster-Scots and Irish language use. The Paulin of a poem such as 'Off the Back of a Lorry' from *Liberty Tree* (1983), with its 'gritty / sort of prod baroque / I must return to / like my own boke', has travelled some way from 'Inishkeel Parish Church'. In changing the terms of the debate about Hardy, Paulin separates himself from the Anglocentricity of the Davie/Larkin axis. And Hardy becomes a fellow-traveller on this journey. 'Funky' language Hardy, dialect, song: these all connect to Paulin's own language preoccupations in Ulster; the 'northern Gothic' obliquely evokes an Anglo-Irish Protestant gothic tradition from Edgeworth to Stoker. He also asserts the margin against the 'centre', a post-colonial reinvigoration of a dying English tradition: Hardy, 'outside' this imperial and institutional centre, thus becomes the bedfellow of Yeats and Joyce, as of Heaney and Paulin – those who took, as Joyce has it in *A Portrait of the Artist as a Young Man*, the language that was not 'theirs', and yet made it their own. To set Hardy's 'provincialism' against Arnold's is to echo Patrick Kavanagh's celebration of the 'parish' as the 'universe'. It is also to conscript Hardy for the backlash against Arnold in Irish Studies in the 1980s, where Arnold comes under fire for his attempt, in *On the Study of Celtic Literature* (1867) at, as Seamus Deane has it, 'killing home rule by kindness'.[34] Since Arnold's book prompted Yeats's defence of Ireland and its traditions in the 1902 essay 'The Celtic Element in Literature', Paulin's new Hardy is also therefore a rather unlikely ally of W.B. Yeats. He draws out the links further:

> Hardy's lines draw profoundly on the folk imagination, and...that imagination overrides the great division between life and death – it locates the resurrection in the self-delighting wildness of sheer rhythm. And this resembles Yeats's remark that passionate rhythm preserves and transforms personal emotion by lifting it out of history into the realm of 'impersonal meditation'. [...] Ultimately,

---

34 See for example the arguments in Seamus Deane, 'Arnold, Burke and the Celts', *Celtic Revivals* (London: Faber, 1985), 17-27.

Hardy is close to Yeats in the connection which he makes between vocal rhythm and mystery... [...] It's as if the muse visits him only when he learns to reject the instrumental will (rhythms of 'choice') for a more intuitive, 'rougher' type of verse which is rooted in rural speech, the Dorset accent and the formally very sophisticated dialect verse of William Barnes. This can only be discovered through a surrender to natural magic and superstition, through a creative idleness rather than a forcing ambition.[35]

Where Larkin's own creative process required the artificial separation of Hardy and Yeats, Paulin's requires their artificial yoking together. Whether or not these sentences are wholly convincing, it's notable that they litter a description of Hardy with Yeatsian terminology and quotation – 'the great division', 'resurrection, 'self-delighting', 'Antaeus-like', 'mystery', 'natural magic' (which is, for Yeats, in 'The Celtic Element in literature', Ireland's 'ancient religion').

IV.

Whether putting the Ulster into Wessex or the Wessex into Ulster, this criticism stands as testament to Hardy's cultural (and political) significance for the Northern Irish writer at a particular moment in history. That significance is also true, in a different way, for Michael Longley and for Seamus Heaney. Longley's 'Poetry', from *The Weather in Japan* (2000), traces the link between Hardy and the poets of the Western Front – among them Edward Thomas – whose influence pervades Longley's own work too: 'When Thomas Hardy died his widow gave Blunden / As memento of many visits to Max Gate / His treasured copy of Edward Thomas's *Poems*.' For Longley, Hardy as love poet subtly inflects Longley's own marital love poems; his 'Mayo Monologues' cross Kavanagh's influence with Hardy; and as one of the outstanding elegists of his generation, for whom the Great War protest-elegy looms large in his own development, Hardy's refiguring of elegy affects Longley's own practice, even if at one remove. For Heaney, as Tara Christie persuasively demonstrates, his 'fifty-year engagement with the works of Thomas Hardy has played a central, complex, and every-changing role in Heaney's poetic vision'. It is, she argues 'perhaps because Hardy entered Heaney's imagination so early

---

35 Paulin, *Thomas Hardy*, 2nd ed., 9, 10-11.

on, because his influence was so intimately and seamlessly blended into Heaney's poetic vision from its outset, that Hardy's presence in Heaney's poetry has gone largely unnoticed. For Hardy has never *not* been a part of Heaney.'[36]

For Heaney, Hardy's parish, like Kavanagh's, makes its own importance: the two poets connect for him in the formation of his own aesthetic, and in his sensing of place. 'I always' Heaney says, 'felt something familiar about Hardy's landscape, and indeed about the figures in his landscape'.[37] (In *Stepping Stones*, Heaney relates how, on meeting Kavanagh, 'I either commended Thomas Hardy or asked what he himself thought of Hardy, but he was on to me like a shot – suspected I was making too nifty a link between one "country" poet and another...'. [38]) Whilst a lecturer at Queen's University Belfast in the late 1960s, Heaney taught a series of undergraduate seminars on Thomas Hardy. The set text list was as follows:

> *The Return of the Native*
> *The Mayor of Casterbridge*
> *The Woodlanders*
> *Tess of the D'Urbervilles*
> *Selected Poems*
> *Hardy's Love Poems,* ed. Carl Weber

The seminars on Hardy were 'to be concerned with the following topics':

> 1. Character and plot in Hardy's Novels: determined or self-determining?
> 2. Suffering in the novels: scourge or salvation?
> 3. The poetry: culmination of Hardy's vision?[39]

The texts are given in chronological order of publication, but *The Return of the Native* topping the list is serendipitous here. In 'The

36 Tara Christie, 'Seamus Heaney's Hardy', *The Recorder* vol. 17 no. 1 (Summer 2004), 118-19

37 Quoted in Christie, 119.

38 Dennis O'Driscoll, *Stepping Stones: Interviews with Seamus Heaney* (London: Faber, 2008), 73.

39 This information is from a discarded typewritten sheet left in a box in an office in Queen's, and found by Dr Eamonn Hughes in the early 1990s. I am grateful to Dr Hughes for drawing my attention to it, and for sight of the handout.

Birthplace', from *Station Island* (1984), one of three 'tribute' poems to Hardy, the poet remembers how, thirty years previously, he 'read until first light // for the first time, to finish / *The Return of the Native*'. If there is a political resonance to this – given Heaney's comments on Kavanagh's confidence in his parish as a means of bringing 'the subculture to cultural power'[40] – there is also, in the final lines of the poem, an astonishing sense of homecoming for Heaney in Hardy's fiction: 'I heard / roosters and dogs, the very same / as if he had written them'. Elsewhere, he describes how Hardy's 'The Oxen' was learnt 'by heart early on....the words "barton" and "coomb" seemed to take me far away and at the same time to bring me close to something lurking inside me. Then there was the phrase, "their strawy pen", which had a different familiarity, it brought the byre and the poetry book into alignment.'[41]

A 'different familiarity' might encapsulate Hardy's appearance in two poems from *Seeing Things* (1991), 'Lightenings vi' and 'vii'. In them, we find a Hardy who makes sense to Heaney, who, like himself, is a poet whose roots cross with his reading, whose rural background in all its sensuous immediacy is the foundation on which he will later 'sing' the 'perfect pitch' of himself:

> Once, as a child, out in a field of sheep,
> Thomas Hardy pretended to be dead
> And lay down flat among their dainty shins.

> In that sniffed-at, bleated-into, grassy space
> He experimented with infinity.

This might seem to be a version of the natural, unsophisticated, grounded Hardy, derided by Leavis and Eliot, celebrated, conversely, by Heaney, and a long way from Paulin's gritty, funky, political Hardy. Nevertheless, Heaney here creates his own Hardy too, and for different ends. Heaney's Hardy is also a visionary poet, experimenting with 'infinity', and the poem, as 'Lightenings vii' then shows, finds the visionary ambition in Hardy in part because it misremembers the

---

40 Seamus Heaney, in *Reading the Future: Irish Writers in Conversation with Mike Murphy* (Dublin: Lilliput Press, 2000), 84-5.

41 Seamus Heaney, interview with John Brown, *In the Chair: Interviews with Poets from the North of Ireland* (Ireland: Salmon Publishing, 2002), 77.

anecdote (in fact, 'He went down on all fours...sought the creatures face to face'.) As Tara Christie points out, Hardy's childhood, through the misremembering, thus merges with Heaney's own, in which Heaney would visit the cattle-shed, to sit or stand 'quietly beside these big peaceful beasts, wondering if they were taking any heed of me or not'.[42] Similarly, 'The Birthplace', while returning Hardy to his origins, also makes him resonate in a new context. Section I is obliquely evocative of Yeats, with the 'stir' of Hardy's 'reluctant heart', as it echoes early Mahon too, the Mahon of 'The Studio' or 'Courtyards in Delft' ('The deal table where he wrote, so small and plain, / the single bed a dream of discipline...'). The line break after 'That day, we were like one' momentarily implies the two poets' affinity, only to transform the speaker into a (suffering) character in one of Hardy's novels: 'like one / of his troubled couples, speechless / until he spoke for them'. The poem allows 'Hardy' (Hardy the novelist, also the Hardy of 'The Voice') to articulate Heaney, all the while speaking both to and for Hardy, Heaney simultaneously creating a character of his own. And the opening of section III – 'Everywhere being nowhere / who can prove / one place more than another?' – is not so much a denial of specificity but a recognition that Hardy, like Heaney after him, has 'proved' a particular place, be it 'Wessex' or Anahorish, against those who would dismiss it as insignificant – to the extent that it can become, at least for Heaney, an imagined realm – '[u]tterly empty', as he has it in the 'Clearances' sequence of *The Haw Lantern* (1987), 'utterly a source'.

In Edna Longley's *Bloodaxe Book of 20th-Century Poetry* (2000), Hardy and Yeats stand at the beginning of the century. The very first poem in that anthology – Hardy's 'The Darkling Thrush' – defines both a century's end and its beginning, and is evoked by Heaney in his own 'millennium' poem quoted as epigraph to this essay. Longley's opening remarks on Hardy encapsulate the shape of critical recognition owed on both sides of the Irish sea: 'Thomas Hardy anticipates every crossroads of modern poetry in the British Isles. He stands between folk-traditions and literature; region and metropolis; Christianity and the post-Darwinian crisis of faith; Victorian and modern consciousness; prose-fiction and poetry; "things [that] go

42 See Christie, 'Seamus Heaney's Hardy', 131-2.

onward the same" and modern war.'[43] It is apparent, even looking briefly at his reception in England and Ireland, that Hardy is different things to different people: Eliot's Hardy is not Larkin's, or Paulin's, or Heaney's Hardy. In standing at a 'crossroads' he leads in multiple directions, and the danger is that in being at once everywhere he is fully appreciated nowhere. Yet more positively, the closing lines of Heaney's 'Lightenings vi' might serve as metaphor for Hardy's reaching 'outward' in terms of influence, as well as being returned to his proper 'place' in the criticism of modern poetry:

> ...that stir he caused
> In the fleece-hustle was the original
>
> Of a ripple that would travel eighty years
> Outward from there, to be the same ripple
> Inside him at its last circumference.

---

43 Edna Longley, ed. *The Bloodaxe Book of 20th Century Poetry from Britain and Ireland* (Tarset: Bloodaxe, 2000), 25.

HARRY CLIFTON

THREE POEMS

Larkin in Belfast

An attic overlooking Elmwood Avenue,
Bedroom, livingroom, bathroom, galley kitchen –
Peace at last, between religions,
Free of the binary. And the writing you do

In the after-hours of social conscience
No-one's hostage. Nothing above you
But mountain, Irish cloud. The women who love you
Safely overseas, at an ideal distance –

Loughborough, London, Leicester... Good years, then.
Not, of course, that you know it at the time.
That comes later. Blue, blue skies, great fame,
A future perfect, without gods or men.

HARRY CLIFTON

Bangor 1944

Not since the Flight of the Earls
Had such a fleet gathered.
There was business in the great world
Any day now. It would take them south

Before that summer's fife and drums,
On a tide for France.
Meanwhile, jazz and chewing-gum,
A girl's lost innocence...

The town awoke, one day. They had gone.
That was seventy years ago
And nothing has happened since,

No life, no death. And nothing won
Or lost. Time in suspension,
Empire, weal and woe.

HARRY CLIFTON

The Place of Stonings

Here the accounts diverge. The written word
Can only go so far, before dissolving
In unhistorical haze.... And the dead are no help

Who came that day through the trees, and saw the mountains
Spread before them, like a lost ideal
They were singing of, the marchers and stewards

Coming, ever so slowly, round the bend,
To be stoned, descended on
By God's right hand, his eggs in a single basket,

Before vanishing, who had given up on themselves
Long ago, into an image of justice,
A future where the trees, the road remain,

And forty years go by, empty of anything
But gossip at a crossroads,
Feathergrass singing, mountains lost in rain.

JOHN MCAULIFFE

TWO POEMS

Part of the Furniture

The door handles are stiff and squeak;
an old rug fades in the light.
We empty a wardrobe, remove
a photo, files, a book she wanted,
and look around. The décor
is suddenly apparent, styles
that came and went, colours going
as late light pours,
through the landing window,
into what used to be your room
which we see only as it marks us.
No guessing, until we saw it,
that the child's rocking chair
lent, decades ago, by a neighbour,
would take on this heavy, amber permanence,
creaking, as soon as you touch it,
to and from a future
the day already darkens.

JOHN MCAULIFFE

House at Night

Because there's no one else around
you like the house at night.
Silent phones, a blank screen,
cherry blossom edging
the extra hour. Nothing to do.
No one's going to call.

                Spring,
a forgotten pocket you dip into,
turns up a late ray of light
across your mouth
and neck.
House at night, last
a little longer!

GARY ALLEN

THREE POEMS

Mayflies

That was the summer The Stranglers played the Arcadia Ballroom
I copped-off with the groupie up from Belfast to sleep with Cornwell,
on the slow country train we shared chewing-gum and beer

and it was hot, as early summers were hot
with the smell of dried-out fields and carriage seats
skinheads flicking and carving with knives
children crying, vibrating floors sticky with vomit

somnolent cows at gates watching us going by
the slow rumination of sapless cud –

I saw them last year, that's when I met Cornwell
we slept in the best hotel. And I could smoke
from a stack on the table, like a real rock bitch,
I wonder, I suppose he'll still remember me...

her sing-song voice irritating like the links of a train
bouncing up and down like the beads of sweat on her breasts.

The station but one from the coast
the doors open, breathless heat
concrete, diesel, iron, time passing

a tense whistle, and I think
of Whitsun Weddings and High Windows
and casual sex by a familiar childhood sea, denied to me

and a young face already perceived to be old
with lines and a long day's bad make-up

the under-smell of sweat masked by cheap perfume
how time fills out a space, where everything is lived
and dies in a day no one quite remembers

like the caravans with their makeshift lines of washing
the bungalows and B&B's, fed-up families
going back to sprawling estates
with tinny radios and sand-filled shoes
the encompassing silence within the train
like the rows of burnt-out double-deckers already cold.

GARY ALLEN

Five points

I dream borders, red map lines
running through frozen pine forests
snow peaked mountain ranges
black Bogland, dilapidated hill farms cut in two
mail trains carrying diseases along veins
and broken lungs as we sleep.

My father could wallow in the distance beneath his eyes
fight a war without understanding the morality
could never find the deserts he fought in on any map –
he found me a large atlas in a rubbish skip
hard blue cloth covers
psychical features of unknown lands
in brown, green, and blue contours

even then, I knew things had changed
that borders had been pushed aside by suffering
the sun had set on Manchuria
the Tsar's brains made mosaics on a wall in Ekiterinburg
Musil died while exercising and the Franz Liszt
steamed and rolled from Budapest to Vienna
Ireland deep as a berry like a quarter of the world:

still, I could dream, a puppeteer residing above people
who were there, yet were no longer there
I could still see burning villages, men on horseback –

where are you now my mother?
lost in uncharted lands
a girl again, who thought the border
was a real presence, a dry stone wall, a ditch.

My father climbed over his own death in cruel pain

my aunt lay back into hers with a gasp
but my mother became a child again
walking miles into the clicking of a respirator.

And I dream a nightmare country
a station beneath pointless far-off stars
where migrants wait on wooden benches in waiting-rooms
and khaki soldiers sleep along the track humped like dead whales

and my mother is young again
a young woman without human boundaries
who has found love in a strange place.

GARY ALLEN

The Picture Show

The first film I ever saw was *A Hard Day's Night*
but the songs were already old when it reached our town
and the Civil Rights marches hadn't even begun

the girls singing out of tune in the back stalls
would have their arms broken
by men with iron bars and chain

as my mother and aunt shared a forbidden cigarette
stolen from my father's coat pocket
as the usherette sold mouldy chocolate
the thin beam of her torch separating lovers

and we grew bored and longed for Fu Manchu –
Look at Ringo, he grew up on a poor street in Liverpool,
just like us

like the teenagers in shirts and thin ties and quiffs
hanging round the toilet lights
drinking half bottles of wine

as our bums itched with flea bites
the floor beneath our feet sticky with vomit and piss
like blood from noses and ears and head wounds
of students falling like lambs into ditches

my mother and aunt screamed and shook their heads
and my young brother woke and bawled
till the manager in a dancehall suit
came down and shooed us to the exit

then someone made tea, and bandages from torn shirts
and some stood for the Queen
my mother and aunt embarrassed on a wet matinee street –
after all, they were only girls looking for idols.

FRED POLLACK

TWO POEMS

Lips and Eyes

I wish I could write love-poems.
Some people write only love-poems.
Instead I philosophise.
I think the appeal of love-poems,
love aside, is to show you've arrived.
That you're not merely feeling, yearning, wanking,
but *doing*. Some poets, guys even,
keep it up long into marriage –
they escape crib and kitchen
to write poems about their wives.
Well I love my wife but keep quiet
so as not to tempt the Demiurge,
who loves to deprive us of happiness
and can't be philosophized.
If I wrote instead of old girl-friends,
my wife would look at me cross-eyed –
unless, perhaps, I omitted
all trace of the erotic.
Described the ones who left me
for lack of financial, genetic,
or entertainment potential.
Or the ones I left, hysterical
because I hate to hurt women
and thereby hurt them more.
It's always possible to learn
something new, however cold
and shrivelled, in the cracks
of what you learned earlier.

FRED POLLACK

The Poetry of Empire

We were taking a course in the Poetry
of Empire. But so swift
is change in today's world that the Empire
collapsed at midterm.
Students from the new Empire
(they spat, talked in class,
despised the work and anyone
not themselves) quit.
Students from prior Empires
greeted the change as yet another
sardonic, predictable and predicted
allegory, and stayed.
 I, from a mere Culture – with
the wit that replaces a past, a passport
stamped by my torturers, someone's couch
to sleep on, skill at hunger,
and hope for a nicer couch – stayed

because I like the material.
The Poetry of Empire is spacious,
generous. Through it one sees
the poet's house, neat or charmingly
dishevelled. A sleeping child,
and the child eating. Beyond that child,
a career and amours.
Beyond the lawn, a car,
and another, beyond the husband another.
A vast buffet, if one tunnels past
irrelevancies! This poetry
reminds me of my Culture's, which is all love –
vertiginous love for a queenly, disdainful,
in fact all-powerful woman whom,
tunnelling, one can see

weeping and mutilated
in a dark room.
But when I said as much
to our prof, a man of the Empire, he shook
his graying pony-tail,
dismayed that someone like me, as black
and wise as night, should praise Empire
over Culture.
Unalarmed or unaware
that his Empire was no longer there,
and that he himself must sink
from sensitivity to pain, he seemed
day by day more ethereal
to us who remained.
He will survive like a verse,
this one: "It is not for me
to grade, to teach you, but for you to teach me!"
– in one breath begging
love and a curse.

BRIDGET MEEDS

TWO POEMS

It's Not What You Mean But What You Say

I know this couple in the city who are hearing but speak sign language.
Sometimes they play this game where she pretends she is deaf
and he signs everything for her. This is when she is feeling shy.
She cannot taste or smell, the result of a childhood accident.
Astonished, I watch her reduce her remaining senses.
She relinquishes her voice and ears with fetching ease.

When he translates, his fingers fly furiously, wedding ring sparking gold.
That time he blackened her eye ("So clumsy!" she said),
he cried for days. Her purple bruise was beautiful in a complicated way.
She wore sunglasses indoors, smiled carefully, and avoided mirrors.
All she would keep is touch: she would be senseless
but for his hand on her arm, guiding her through the terrifying crowds.

BRIDGET MEEDS

The Peaches Stolen From My Tree

I step outside with morning chores to do
and find the peach tree lightened, overnight,
of its heady, fuzzy, rose-cheeked freight.
Am I not a woman who'd tuck into
the crop of peaches in her fenced-in yard?
I would have sliced them into chilled white wine;
perhaps your hunger was more fierce than mine.
I am too busy a wife to stand guard.
But as a girl I also stole, wanting
the sweetness of another, brought the sun-
warmed fruit to my lips, licked its juicy swell.
The tree stretches, ignoring me, flaunting
freedom from fruit and our desires, undone.
It eyes the sky, the false asphodel.

DIANE FAHEY

THREE POEMS

Spring Mornings

After the first hours, spent tuning poems,
I rise, step round skewed bundles of papers
and start, methodically, to build the day.
The table set, I'll go to call you from sleep,
may find you like a wakeful child, waiting
to be saved from pain, or aloneness –
your breath laboured as a swimmer's in tall waves.
Rice cakes and jam, porridge, pills, tea.
In the garden, later, I'll massage your neck
while sunlight bathes your face, thin arms.
We'll take stock: violets, white and blue,
monbretias; soon, the irises.
All's well.
Curved in on themselves, mind, body,
start to unfurl. *This freshness.*

Diane Fahey

Snapshot

'All the world is green'
   – Tom Waits

2.15, mid-week, mid-spring.
We're in the green armchairs, looking out
at the hardenburgia – its sunstruck,
nodding leaves a shadow-play
on the window's wire screen; through a tear
one leaf grows in towards us, patterned by
the netting's grid, other leaf-tongues.
Tom Waits is singing, wants everything
to be fresh again; to forgive,
be forgiven – while the world's clock grinds on,
half-ironically, in the background.
Two quiet souls. Increasingly you love
this dusky stillness... Now you're off to bed.
I write the poem. The music ends.

DIANE FAHEY

Connections

I write few poems now, in thrall to your
perilous decline. Still prone to humour
you snipe, 'Speak in English next time!'
after I've shouted to your deafness
down the phone, my hand cupped, as if round
one of those jam-tins linked by string,
known to us both in childhoods, worlds away.
You're present in the fit of my flesh;
no doubt you still can feel me at your body's core.
New life: a secret permeating its host,
getting ready to reveal... Who knows
what death is?
Afterwards, you'll live
in the cells of my memory, forever
hanging up that phone in amused disgust.

DONAL MAHONEY

TWO POEMS

Mostly Basie with a Little Bach

Whenever I see a new woman, I know
I should look at her hair and her eyes and her smile
before I decide if she's worth the small talk
and the dinner later
and whatever else she may require
before she becomes taffy,
pliant and smiling.
But that never works for me.
Whenever I see a new woman,
what matters to me is never
her hair or her eyes or her smile;

what matters to me is her saunter
as I stroll behind her.
If her moon comes over the mountain
and loops in languor, left to right,
and then loops back again,
primed for another revolution, then
I introduce myself immediately
no matter where we are,
in the stairwell or on the street
and that's when I see for the first time
her hair and her eyes and her smile
but they are never a distraction since
I'm lost in the music of her saunter.

Years ago, tall and loping Carol Ann
took a train to Chicago,
found a job and then one summer day

walked ahead of me on Michigan Avenue
while I surveyed her universe amid
the cabs screeching, horns beeping,
a driver's middle finger rising.
Suddenly she turned and said hello
and we shook hands and I saw her smile
dart like a minnow and then disappear
as she frowned and asked
why was I walking behind her.

I told her I was on my way to the noon Mass
at Holy Name Cathedral and she was welcome
to come along. The sermon wouldn't be much,
I said, but the coffee and bagels afterward
would be plentiful, enough to cover lunch.
And Jesus Christ Himself would be there.
She didn't believe me, not at all,
and she hasn't believed me since.

That was thirty years ago and now
her smile is still a minnow
darting here and there but now
it's more important than her saunter
which is still a symphony,
mostly Basie with a little Bach.

And I no longer traipse Michigan Avenue
as I did years ago looking for new moons
swirling in my universe. Instead,
I take my lunch in a little bag
on a long train from the suburbs
and I marvel at one fact:
It's been thirty years since I first heard
the music in her saunter
and Carol Ann and I are
still together, praise the Lord.
Who can believe it? Not I.
Carol Ann says she knew
the ending from the start.
Lord, Almighty. Fancy that.

DONAL MAHONEY

The Whole Mad Swirl

with my thanks to MH Clay

I was out of control, spinning
on the whirligig of youth,
giddy to be caught
in what Kerouac called
"the whole mad swirl
of everything to come."
I didn't know what to expect.
I was ready for nothing
though I had spent years
in solitary confinement

with books, exams and degrees.
You would think I'd have
learned
something about life as it is,
not as I wished it to be.
I went out on the street
to look for work
and was surprised to discover
no one spoke Old English
like Beowulf or Middle English
like the Wife of Bath.

An old professor told me
I talked the way
e.e. cummings wrote
and no one would hire me.
A few years later I married
a woman with several degrees.
She thought I was normal.
We had five kids in six years
and drove landlords bonkers.
"The Lord will provide,"

we said, and He did.
Fifty years later, the five kids
have rucksacks of their own
packed with jobs, marriages,
children and good lives
measured against
the standard of most.
Their mother is dead,
and like everyone else
on this strange planet

I am in the process
of dying in the jaws
of what Kerouac called
"the whole mad swirl
of everything to come."
I have seen almost all
of "everything to come"
except for the best part
and that, I am told,
will take my breath away.

John Wheway

Three Poems

Laundry

Deciding to peg out my wash, I fasten
every button on each shirt, tug

the seams straight to minimise ironing,
something you wouldn't have bothered with.

Between the washing-line and the shed roof
my duvet-cover flaps like a full sail.

Upstairs, I decide to unstuff
the airing-cupboard where you bundled

bedlinen, towels, curtains, those Greek
beach blankets with indelible sun-oil -

all so jumbled, I start to lose myself.
I sort things into categories, make

five neat piles on the shelves - that's how I find
the sheet with the stains

from those cherries I squashed between your lips
that first afternoon.

John Wheway

Blind Man's Buff

When it's Grandma's turn to be it,
it's not because of her wooden leg

that the grown-ups want her to be exempt,
but because they know her technique

with a walking stick – they've felt
its crack across shoulder-blades

buttocks, skulls, knuckles –
blows they weren't quick enough to duck.

That's why, when she reaches for the blindfold,
her firstborn son offers her instead

a new-opened bottle of India pale ale –
to oppose her will with temptation.

Grandma tightens the knot, turns
on her heel, firms up her grip –

foam erupts from the bottle's neck, trails
the length of a Lancer's spear on the label,

the silence marked as each drop hits the ground –
drip, after drip, after drip.

JOHN WHEWAY

Amphetamine Mom

She was so all over the place, she left
her purse open on the kitchen table

or on sofa cushions;
a big mouth with brass lips,

its satin throat shadowed with folds and cavities,
valuables hidden deep in a belly

of grainy pigskin – dyed pale beige,
the same colour as the fake suntan

she smoothed on her legs in summer,
centering an eyebrow-pencil line

down the backs of her calves
for the illusion of nylons.

The first time he dipped inside
he didn't pinch the pills, but dared himself

to finger them until she was twisting the doorknob.
He pulled out just in time to hide

his hand – powdery, with that funny smell.
In his pocket he chirred marbles –

he tried to slow his breathing, to show her
the look of innocence she needed.

Stop that racket, she spat, *it sets
my teeth on edge.*

NIALL CAMPBELL

Later Tasting

Who knows what he meant by that first-last gift
of grit and pollen and sheep-dirt, and rain,
and whatever was on the hand that picked them:
diesel, linen soap, fish blood, with peat crumbs
not emptied from the picking bucket.
The berries sieved beneath the garden pump.

Now pot, now jam-sugar and upper heat
and soon the felt cream lifted off, too sweet,
too sour, for tasting.
                    Bees strike against
the kitchen glass; nectar birds stall in the air
somewhere in their dark jungles. My grandfather,
knowing what a mouth is for, watches it cool

then asks to hold the bundle of his grandchild
and feeds this less-than-one year old, this milk child,
one teaspoon, and it shivers through the taste.

Today, I find another jar – still red
as a letter seal – and find it sweet, so sweet,
so sweet – and think I nearly understand him.

Remembering Our Wars

Carol Ann Duffy (ed.), *1914: Poetry Remembers*, Faber and Faber, £14.99
Tim Kendall (ed.), *Poetry of the First World War: An Anthology*, Oxford
University Press, £14.99

Ireland is not the only country to have entered a decade of difficult
centenaries. Irish commemoration of that 'time of the breaking of
nations' belongs with wider European and British memorial acts –
including poems. Indeed, as regards the Great War itself, writers have
contributed to making Irish memory less divided. Seamus Heaney,
Michael Longley, Paula Meehan, Bernard O'Donoghue, Paul Muldoon
and Theo Dorgan are among the poets who accepted Carol Ann Duffy's
invitation 'to help *us* [my italics] remember the tragedy of the Great
War by responding in new poems to the poetry, or other texts, which
emerged from those four barbaric years of violence and slaughter;
when Science and Politics became servants to War'.

You don't have to be Michael Gove to find that summary a trifle
simplistic. Duffy also over-simplifies when she calls her anthology a
place where 'the voices of the living and the dead mingle', and thanks
poets 'for their commitment to ensuring that poetry remembers
1914'. These formulations forget that poetry has been 'remembering'
ever since; that, both conceptually and politically, remembrance is
a complex issue; that poets have often recast or invoked precursor-
poems from the war years; that the war poets have hugely influenced
later poetry; that poetry is a unique kind of 'voice'; that its own
structures remain, as Yeats put it, 'shaken by the Great War'. Certainly,
Poetry Remembers does not need the scholarly introductions and
apparatus that make Tim Kendall's new anthology so valuable (at the
same price). But, even if some of the poems fill in some of the blanks,
the Great War requires rather more historical and literary-historical
perspective than Duffy provides.

The pre-texts for these 'new poems' include poems by Apollinaire,
Ungaretti and Akhmatova, as well as by the usual Anglophone
suspects. Poets also draw on letters, memoirs, commentary, and such
diverse testaments as Saki's 'Birds on the Western Front' and Sassoon's

famous statement 'against the political errors and insincerities for which the fighting men are being sacrificed'. The more informal or less formed sources generally provide greater room for creative manoeuvre. For instance, it's hard for any poet to 'respond' to Owen's 'The Send-Off' (reworked by Duffy as a love poem) without being overwhelmed by cadences that symbolise infinite loss. Paraphrase is one sign of being overwhelmed. Ruth Padel pointlessly versifies Saki: 'a wee hen-chaffinch flitted wistfully to and fro, amid splintered and falling branches that had never a green bough left in them' becomes: 'you watched the chaffinch fluttering to and fro / through splintered branches, breaking buds / and never a green bough left'. Similarly, Polly Clark's forced marine metaphor adds nothing to Vera Brittain's disturbing account of casualties during 'wild November' rain: 'In my nurse's uniform I swim among fresh / failures of the broken earth … Most soon drift to the sea-bed'. A related tendency is over-determined pity and horror. Dorgan's 'A Munster Fusilier on his Eightieth Birthday' resorts to horrific listing ('the body / gone down forever under in mud, shit, / blood, bone, viscera and loam'), which nevertheless pales before Robert Graves's 'Dead Boche': 'Dribbling black blood from nose and beard'. A different kind of overkill leads Clare Pollard to link 'blood-smeared' childbirth with the prospect of the male baby dying in war. Deryn Rees-Jones handles a personal parallel more successfully in a poem which identifies her own widowhood with Helen Thomas's grief. It's not that you have to be there ('trench poems' are no longer viewed as the sole mode of Great War poetry): rather, to quote the title of a Second World War poem by Henry Reed, it's a matter of 'Judging Distances'. By the same token, whatever its intrinsic merit, a poem can appear too distant or oblique. Paul Muldoon's 'Dromedaries and Dung Beetles' ostensibly takes off from Brooke's 'The Soldier'. Here 'dung' and a narrative of frontier-less desert travel (beetles being as peripatetic as camels) ironises 'some corner of a foreign field'. But the narrative occupies most of the poem; while war, including a reference to 'Private Henry Muldoon', seems an afterthought as opposed to being put in its unheroic place. And, although Duffy mentions this poem as one marked by 'vivid family connections', it's Google that has connected the poet with Private Muldoon: a Gallipoli casualty from Burnley. Paul Muldoon's earlier poem 'Truce', of course, immortally 'remembers' the war in the context of the Troubles.

Family history vivifies Jackie Kay's 'Bantam' and Roy Fisher's 'Signs and Signals'. Kay, recalling her father recalling his father, makes the word 'wee' count as rarely before in a Scots poem: 'It wisnae men they sent tae war, / It wis boys like the Bantams / – wee men named efter / a small breed o' chickens'. Fisher's poem begins with a powerful 'dead Boche' image – a 'singularly tall / German officer, set upright in the earth / as if in a raised niche' – filtered through the recollection of 'Lance-Corporal (signals) Fisher W., Royal / Fusiliers'. It ends with a more inconsequential 'sign', which suggests this brief poem's scope:

> Then on sunny days
> the pleasure of making the sharp flashes of his heliograph
> go skittering over the filth for miles.

Fisher's source-text is 'Grodek': a poem by Georg Trakl that alludes to 'grandsons yet unborn'. Julia Copus's 'Any Ordinary Morning' also crosses genealogical lines by evoking her husband's great-grandfather, a German casualty 'who shaped my life'. This poem redirects the fragile 'ordinariness' of Edward Thomas's 'As the team's head-brass': it's a nice touch that light 'flashes out', not from 'head-brass', but from a 'silver Kaffeekanne'. Detailed dialogue with sources is comparatively rare. But Billy Collins defuses any presumption in taking on Owen's 'Futility' by making that poem his subject, by glossing its symbolism: 'John Donne tells the sun where to go, / Blake's flower is busy counting its steps ...' In calling his own poem 'Futility', Collins also implies that 'futility', like entropy, increases. Alan Jenkins is the poet who 'responds' most intricately. 'The Jumps' is based on the language of a love letter sent by T.E. Hulme from a shelled war zone. Hulme likens the lovers' limbs to 'interlacing fingers' and calls 'our bodies and legs ... a sort of web or shield, made safe for the time being'. Jenkins's finale darkly combines love and war as soldiers' ghosts 'advance // Towards their girls, all lying there / In fields of wheat or barley', until

> in full view
> Of owl and fox, they kneel, and stare –
> And then what shields, what interlacings!

'The Jumps' alludes to Hulme's aesthetics: 'Nothing "dry, hard" anywhere / Except in iron rows'. Rachel Boast's fine 'The Testament of Jean Cocteau' centres on the relation between art and war:

> From Apollinaire' star-shaped head wound
> grew your signature, flower of shrapnel,
> mercurial flower, the fatal hurt of a moment's fire

bursting into life– for such is art, and such
the calligram of its five petals of resistance
seeping into the edge of an age ...
This poem recognises that the poetics, as well as wounds, of the Great
War remain open. Despite his denials, Owen exemplifies the war
poets' 'concern with poetry'. David Harsent's arresting 'Armistice'
renews Owen's consonantal rhyme (every line ends in a 'd' sound)
for an ironical vision of a 'Peacable Kingdom': 'the dead // silence
that draws out over battlefield and potter's field / is what remains
of the truth of it and must be left unsaid'. Kendall rightly points out
that Modernist critical bias 'overlooks the Georgian origins of most
surviving [Anglophone] war poetry'. But 'Georgian' (an insult rather
than a category) does not suggest the multiple ways in which poets re-
formed 'traditional forms'.

So too, with traditional tropes: 'new poems' continue the long history
of oxymoronic 'war pastoral' – battlefield / potter's field. Bernard
O'Donoghue's 'Migration' begins with the doomed Francis Ledwidge,
author of 'Serbia', 'building a lake-side road like the back-road /
along the Boyne to Swynnerton from Slane'. Seamus Heaney's 'In
a field' evokes a 'tractor with its hoisted plough' and the return of a
rural war-veteran. Here Heaney (who might have been made to do
so) updates 'As the team's head-brass' less obliquely than Copus. In
this context, Adam Horowitz's rather obvious 'Stopping with a bicycle
on a hill above Stroud, thinking of Ivor Gurney' is trumped by Simon
Armitage's 'Avalon', which relocates Gurney's unstable monologue in
San Francisco: 'I straddle each earthquake, one foot either side / of
the faultline, rocking the world's seesaw'. The world also seesaws in
Ann Gray's 'March 2013', which wonderfully responds to Charlotte
Mew's 'Spring, 1915' by quoting an Afghan taxi-driver: 'We have snow
leopards, wild goats, gray wolves ... Three decades of war / but our
foothills still flower'. The last line comes as a shock: 'He winds down
his window – / The Cambridge Backs, massed with purple crocus'. War
pastoral also crops up in the poems (usually closer to contemporary
war zones) that feature in the current issue of the American journal
Prairie Schooner. The poet and Iraq-veteran Brian Turner has guest-
edited an interesting 'War Portfolio', which includes 'A Round Table'

on war writing. Nature and 'beauty' are among the topics discussed. Matt Gallagher, another Iraq veteran, says: 'When individuals are exposed to the very worst of humanity on a daily basis, where else can they turn for relief and solace but the natural world that surrounds them?'

What of new protest beyond an implicitly 'anti-war' message? Gray's taxi-driver says: 'I want my girls to have an education'. Similarly, Imtiaz Dharker twists Owen's 'Doomed Youth' to applaud the bravery of Malala and other schoolgirls who 'stand up / to take their places on the front line'. From another angle, Blake Morrison's 'Redacted', which begins 'This poem has been redacted' and contains blacked-out words, attacks an MOD inquest / cover-up re 'the death of a serving officer' in Afghanistan. This poem well matches Ewart Alan Mackintosh's wartime satire 'Recruiting': 'Lads, you're wanted. Come and die.' It's Andrew Motion who nominates Sassoon's 'statement'. His own poem, which imagines Archduke Franz Ferdinand's consciousness on the day of the Sarajevo assassination, encodes ecological protest in depicting the victim as himself a hunter: a 'mind ... stuffed / with an almost infinite number of ghosts / of woodcock, quail, pheasant and partridge ...' Here an unacknowledged precursor-poem is Thomas's 'The Gallows' (1916), where a game-keeper's gibbet symbolises all human violence.

Although 2014 has hardly begun, new war-books are pouring forth, old debates being recycled. Some kind of war between historiography and poetry has also broken out. Kendall is acutely alive to the politics of the Great War anthology, which began during the war itself. He notes a danger of Owen's later pre-eminence: that it 'established exclusionary principles'. The canon gradually expanded to include less obvious 'war poetry' (Thomas's whole oeuvre); poetry by women who served as nurses or in other roles; poems by male and female civilians – not only established poets. Distinctions between war poetry and war verse (which abounded) became blurred or deplored. Twenty years ago, Martin Stephen's anthology *Poems of the Great War* pre-empted Gove by urging the extent to which patriotic sentiments were 'typical or representative'. The war has also been 'alternatively' anthologised from left-wing and feminist angles. Kendall, who includes far fewer poets than Stephen, gives firm priority to the aesthetic: 'I have interpreted my editorial role as being to arrange the best poems in the best order'. It may or may not be coincidental that 'the best poems' mostly seem to have been written by soldier poets and by women poets with direct experience (Mary Borden, May Sinclair, May Wedderburn Cannan). Yet Kendall enriches the aesthetic hinterland by giving due weight to three civilian poets: Hardy, Kipling and Wilfrid Gibson. The army turned Gibson down, but his empathetic projections were influential: 'We ate our breakfast lying on our backs / Because the shells were screeching overhead ...'.

War-poetry wars will continue: is it Anglocentric of Kendall to include Arthur Graeme West but not Ledwidge or Patrick MacGill? Should he represent Yeats by more than the usual two poems? Would a really rigorous anthology exclude all women poets except, perhaps, Margaret Postgate Cole's beautiful 'Afterwards'? 'What use / To have your body lying here / In Sheer, underneath the larches?'

We still inhabit 'Afterwards'. *The Prairie Schooner Round Table* harks back to Great War poetry (and The Iliad). In the 'After War' issue of *Granta* Patrick French reflects on a problematic family legacy: the heroic militarism of an Irish Catholic relative who died at Mons. No less relevant to Northern Ireland, however, is 'The Rainy Season': an essay in which Lindsey Hilsum disturbingly tells how Rwandan memorial practices are designed to produce amnesia: 'The Ethnographic Museum had been purged of all reference to ethnicity.' Perhaps Carol Ann Duffy should have rejected some of the poems she commissioned. But her anthology makes the point that poetry, the opposite of amnesia, remembers our wars in indelible and indispensable ways.

EDNA LONGLEY

Little Thunder Palaces

Guillaume Apollinaire, *The Little Auto*
(translated by Beverley Bie Brahic). CB Editions, £7.99.

While Yeats was discovering the labour involved in being beautiful
and Eliot decreeing that modern poetry had to be difficult, across the
Channel Wilhelm Albert Włodzimierz Apolinary Kostrowicki was
teaching modernist poetry to be lovable above all else. Is there a more
sheerly delightful, more playfully inventive twentieth-century poet
than Guillaume Apollinaire, as he became? Apollinaire is the original
cubist cabaret singer, all *Gemütlichkeit* and vibrato one minute and
all shock-of-the-new photomontage and post-decadent absinthe
hangover the next.

He was also a war poet, retired from active service with a shrapnel
wound in 1916, but not before bringing the surrealist revolution to
the front line, comparing exploding shells to champagne bottles and
delivering sarcastic paeans to the 'virility of the present century'.
Trench walls reminded him of nougat and breasts were 'the only
bombs that I love'. It was the flu that carried him off in the end, just
before the appearance of the visual *blagues of Caligrammes* and all
the clock-melting surrealist fun of the 1920s on which he so sadly
missed out. By the 1930s, Beckett was describing the *Chanson du mal
aimé* as 'worth the whole of the best of Merril, Moréas, Viéle-Griffin,
Spire, Régnier, Jammes put together', and in 1950 he made good on
his enthusiasm with one of his single best translations, of *Zone*. His
English-language apotheosis was nicely in hand.

In *The Little Auto* Beverley Bie Brahic has concentrated mainly
on later Apollinaire. The title poem describes a car journey from
Deauville to Paris in August 1914 in which 'we bid farewell to a whole
era'. Sniffing political change in the wind, the dogs are howling over
the borders, and Apollinaire breaks into a sinusoidal vispo swoosh I
won't try to reproduce here: 'I shall never forget this journey by night
during which none of us said a word.' Apollinaire was fairly in the
thick of it in what followed (having requested a transfer from Nîmes
to the front), but makes an instructive contrast with the Anglophone

lot. There is no straight opposition between the horrors of war and the pleasures of innocence and vainglory indulged at a safe distance from the *chevaux de frise*. Much of Apollinaire's poignancy derives from the peculiar survival of his innocence behind the lines, his childlike sense of excitement:

> And while the war cry
> Turns the earth bloody
> I hoist the odours
> Beside the colour-savours

> And I sm
>
>> o
>> ke
>> the
>> to
>> bac
>> co
>> of
>> the ZoNE

'Zone' is one of the greatest modern French poems, up there – certainly where its Anglophone readers have been concerned – with *Le cimetière marin* and *Anabase*. It was placed first in *Alcools* despite having been written last, and opens the door to much that would follow in the 1920s and beyond, to Reverdy and Char in French, and Beckett's *Echo's Bones* in English, to go no further. As well as its military connotations, 'zone' suggests a region outside the city walls peopled by transients and immigrants, of whom Apollinaire was one, and whose street life he so memorably paints. The poem's ironic opening panegyric to Pope Pius X is one of the great things in modern poetry, and is reframed by the closing invocation of 'fetishes from Polynesia or Guinea' (Apollinaire's Picasso connection, perhaps). These gods are 'Other Christs with other beliefs / Lesser Christs repositories of obscure faiths', and this is a modernism *minoritaire*, the ethnographic modernism of Hope Mirrlees' *Paris: A Poem* and Nancy Cunard's *Negro Anthology*.

His many friendships with painters and ekphrastic poems are another of the many ways in which Apollinaire resembles Frank

O'Hara (though he planned to title his poems about art not 'Why I
Am Not a Painter' but *Me Too I'm a Painter*). He was also possessed
of O'Haraesque powers of spontaneous overflow, as witness Philippe
Soupault asking him for a poem and receiving 'Ombre' three hours
later. It is a shimmeringly lovely elegy:

> Destinies
> Multiple shadow may the sun watch over you
> You who love me so you never will go away
> Who dance in the sun without kicking up dust
> Ink shadow of the sun
> Script of my light
> Caissons of regrets
> A god who humbles himself

Between *The Little Auto* and her versions of Francis Ponge (*An
Unfinished Ode to Mud*), Brahic has made herself an invaluable
conduit, well on her way to doing for French poetry what Michael
Smith has done for Spanish or Michael Hofmann for German. The
Little Auto is an entirely delightful production, and it is we should
humble ourselves anew before the little 'thunder's palaces' to which
Apollinaire compared his wonderful poems.

DAVID WHEATLEY

"A Songbird's Ribcage Picked Clean"

Sharon Olds, *Stag's Leap*, Cape, £10

The first poetry book I ever bought of my own free will (a teacher did not tell me to buy it) and with my own money (not shoved at me at holiday time) was Sharon Olds' *Satan Says*, her first book, published in 1980. The book contains many fine poems about motherhood, her Calvinist father, abuse, and sex told most often with a violence of feeling. This vivid and piercing debut ends with 'Prayer', a poem that alternates images of birth with images of sex: "the terrible fear / as the child's head moves down into the vagina," "he took his body like a saw to me," "the hot needle of / milk piercing my nipple." By alternating these descriptions, Olds blurs the border between pleasure and pain, between herself and these other, needy bodies. She ends the poem with the prayer of the title, "let me not forget: / each action, each word / taking its beginning from these." This commitment to the body, the *female* body, was breathtaking to the young woman I was. The confessional narrative powered me through a whole poetry book on my own for the first time. I wanted to know what such an honest and angry woman might tell me about being a daughter, wife and mother.

To say that *Stag's Leap*, her most recent book, has been well received is a bit of an understatement; it has been awarded the Pulitzer Prize in America and the T. S. Eliot Prize in the U.K. It is a poem cycle largely written at the time that Olds' husband of thirty years announced that he had fallen in love with someone else and wanted a divorce. For her children's sake, she waited fifteen years to publish the poems, which begin with 'While He Told Me', and end with a section called 'Years Later'. That honest, angry woman I first met years ago has mellowed for better and sometimes, for worse.

The vivid details are still available in *Stag's Leap*, "his deep navel, and the cindery lichen / skin between the male breasts,"('When He Told Me'); "I whispered, Just one / more?, and his indulgent grunt / seemed, to me, to have pleasure," ('Gramercy'); "cancelling twice / when the parasite had come back to my gut," ('Attempted Banquet');

and "you seemed / covered with her, like a child working with glue / who's too young to be working with glue," ('Running Into You'). But I don't find these details to be as eviscerating as in other books. What I love about Olds' usually knife-sharp poems is that through heightened, destabilizing descriptions of lived experience, she opens the door to even scarier statements, the necessarily difficult thoughts a person might express if she were brave enough or if no one was listening. This book, while depending on Olds' usual strategies, is not as fearless.

There are some very fine poems in *Stag's Leap* and, while quieter, they represent an artist at the peak of her skills. For instance, in 'On the Hearth of a Broken Home', the speaker finds two egg shells that have tumbled down the chimney of her house, "one dew-liked / kicked-off slipper of a being now flying," and one that spills a somewhat dried yolk when she lifts it, the "sunrise-milk-green boot of the dead." Olds writes: "[i]f I ever / prayed, as a child, for everlasting / union, these were its shoes." The imagined journey of the two eggs conveys so much more than the details of her reaction to her husband's news, but isn't that the power of metaphor? In 'Approaching Godthab', again, the metaphor is much more powerful than any recounting of lived experience. Olds writes of flying over Greenland,

> [t]he glacierscape called it
> up, the silent, shining tulle,
> the dreaming hats and cubes, the theorems
> and corollaries, that girl who had thought
> a wedding promise was as binding as a law
> of physics. Now I stood outside.

Here Olds wields metaphor with brilliance and power, metaphor the device that pulls in other worlds and engages these worlds to speak for the writer. It's also an opportunity for imagination, especially for a poet such as Olds, engaged as she is in telling the truth about real events in her life.

The parts of the book that speak more directly from the experience of the separation and its aftermath are less affecting or perhaps seem too familiar to be affecting poetry. It's a bit hard to feel it when Olds describes her breasts as she holds them in her hands as "twin widows," or, in her grief, when she writes about the drama of the stains on the car seats, "drool, / tears, ice cream, no wounds, but only / the month's blood of release, and the letting / go when the water broke" ('Pain I Did Not'). Sometimes relationship-speak takes over a poem:

> say there was
> a god—of love—and I'd given—I had meant
> to give—my life—to it—and I
> had failed, well I could just suffer for that—
> but what, if I,
> had harmed, love? ('The Worst Thing')

In these poems, pathos is the end, not some larger, less merely personal experience.

The poet does wonder if all her "telling" over the years of her marriage had become too much for the husband who always seemed a private man—this vein is potentially a rich one to mine, but has not been pushed in this book. And maybe that's why this book doesn't approach its topic with Olds' trademark abandon. Olds has said in an interview that she needs to imagine that those close to her do not read her poems:

> After maybe my second book, my mother saw a poem of mine in a magazine. She called me about it, and I said something like what would really work for me would be to keep family and poetry separate, if I could, and I asked her not to read my poems.[1]

I always want to like Olds' poems and most often do. Indeed, I like many in *Stag's Leap*. The judge's comments for both the Pulitzer and the T.S Eliot Prizes mention the narrative of the collection, the cycle of pain and acceptance through which the speaker passes. For me, too, this was an important part of the book; I wanted to know what happens when a marriage is ended for your by your spouse. The awards speak perhaps about our continued need for stories, human stories. After all these years, after all the modernisms and postmodernisms have burned off their brilliances, maybe we just need to read what happened when a husband told a wife he didn't love her anymore.

CONNIE VOISINE
***
1 http://www.poets.org/viewmedia.php/prmMID/ 22972#sthash.dQ7i1Y8M.dpuf

Neither Plain nor Mannered

Fleur Adcock, *Glass Wings*, Bloodaxe, £9.95
Robin Robertson, *Hill of Doors*, Picador, £9.99

'Dragonfly,' first printed in *The Yellow Nib* (No.7, Spring 2012) gives Fleur Adcock's new collection its beautiful jacket photograph (a Blue Darner Dragonfly from Canada) though not its title. It closes the collection's fourth and final part, a myth-resistant but imaginatively lively set of encounters with the jointed-limbed ones, *My Life with Arthropods*. Adcock's Lake District dragonfly is "a series of blue-green / flashes over Lily Tarn" but also "a contraption of steel and cellophane..." Praying Mantises are "coloured paper cut-outs", the stag beetle "a small black spitfire". Clustered metaphors garnish the poet's favourites, like the spider –"hirsute acorn", "luscious danglers", "furry-trousered velvet raisins" ('Orb Web'). Readers of a certain generation may remember the "Martian" poets.

But the primary concern is not de-familiarisation. For a "people-poet" like Adcock, no arthropod is too good for a personal anecdote. Sometimes a powerful question-mark uncurls between them: 'Crayfish,' connects the "midden-debris" left by a schoolgirl-feast to the anatomical grandeur of the full-grown Rock Lobster. Extinction is an anxiety, though in certain cases it might be welcome. Fleas are embarrassing if fun to "crunch" between thumbnails; crab-lice provide an occasion for an extended risqué joke: "'Crab lice, authors experience of' / is an index entry you won't find / in my not-to-be written memoirs" ('Unmentionable').

'Blowflies', the source of the title's "glass wings", follows lustrous description into withdrawal, as the speaker stops herself from further maggoty imaginings with a coyly curt "but enough - / the others will kindly absent themselves, please!" This inserts a buzzy end-rhyme but mollifies Death's sting. The insect in the room may resemble the poet in the tidy-minded neighbourhood, tactfully challenging convention, amusing but not terrifying broader-minded friends.

Adcock's "memoirs" are her poems. There are three other sections to

Glass Wings: the second, Testators, visits a miscellany of ancestors via their touchingly-modest bequests, and the third, Campbells, opens with a tender elegy for Alistair Campbell, the "beautiful poet" and father of Adcock's children. New Zealand and England complicate Adcock's sense of home, family and arthropod collection, but displacement is countered by a carefully negotiated socialisation, an adaptable vernacular and an address-book of treasured names.

Adcock favours regular stanzaic constructions. Robertson sometimes employs such structures but his poems typically expand as chunkier organisms. In *Hill of Doors* a poem is often alone with unmediated nature. Death's stare is returned: Robertson's lobster, unlike Adcock's, is alive at the start of his poem, but ultimately goes "eyes first / into the fire" ('A Quick Death'). Dynamic rhythms reinforce the often mimetic enterprise, as in 'Corryvreckan', a swirling North Sea brew of rangy sentences and swift abbreviations: "...the sea's so high it's climbing over itself to get through. / They call these 'the overfalls'. A sluice through a bottleneck. / A great seething. The frenzy of water feeding on water". The diction is neither plain nor mannered, and Scots dialect sparingly employed, but English gets a salutary overhaul. Original poems are flanked by translations from Ovid's *Metamorphoses* and from the *Dionysaica*, a Latin epic by the 5th century Greek poet, Nonnus. The sometimes-animal god who endures alternate sacrifice and re-birth, Dionysus also shapes a personal myth. More contemporary encounters with the underworld have an edge-of-seat pace and fundamental moral seriousness recalling Stephen King. The different "annunciations" of both opening and final poems connect a hard-won emergence into light.

While it seems a pity that Adcock chose not to include translations in such a comprehensively biographical collection, both *Glass Wings* and *Hill of Doors* represent their authors at the height of their unique and entirely dissimilar powers.

CAROL RUMENS

Two Psalmists

Nick Laird, *Go Giants*. London: Faber, £12.99
Michael Symmons Roberts, *Drysalter*. London: Cape, £12

Go Giants is a bold collection of poems produced by patient observation and careful attention to the nuance of contemporary speech. The volume – Laird's third – is driven by ire, or what my Sunday School teacher would have called righteous anger. Laird's fist isn't raised to the vacated heavens, but to the fact of death and at those redemptive narratives that elide the story of the gods' departure for a contrary emphasis on redress and transformation. If this sounds grand, even mock-heroic, we also hear the mumbled protestations of a boy enwrapped in a Spiderman quilt, perhaps the son of a man 'killed in his own town by anagrams / of nativist and visitant' ('Progress') in a province addicted to the myth of progress despite the accumulating evidence of its grief and stasis. Language, too, connives in death dealing.

Go Giants looks from out from a lower Manhattan high-rise, an art gallery in Rome and a kitchen table in London to reflect, with subtle intelligence, on the appetites, politics, noise and boredom of contemporary life. It looks, from each, to the once Troubled north and the area around Cookstown – specifically its cemetery, school, church and meatplant. Here, 'porn mags stashed in blackthorn hedges' ('Progress') are a familiar feature of the landscape, and traumatic memories return despite the attempt to focus on the Celestial City whether it appears as a promised peaceful future or in the suburban bliss of 'central heating / and four / triangles of buttered toast' ('Observance'). The targets of Laird's critique of the myth of progress are varied: Apollonian logic, Faith School curricula, neoliberal promises or the old-fashioned evangelical revival tent of 'The Mission', where the speaker stands by, 'watching Ryan crying like a little baby / as he stumbles down towards the stage to testify and get saved'. These are intelligent and emotional poems that make knowing use of cliché and colloquialism. We are shown 'some treeless / crossroads in the back end / of nowhere', made suddenly famous, 'then synonymous with loss' ('Collusion').

In 'The Mark', one of my favourite poems from the volume, the cool interiors of an art museum prompt a sustained reflection on scapegoating, suffering and the ethics of ekphrasis. Learning from Auden's 'Musée des Beaux Arts', Laird's description of the marble that shows Marsyas, cheated by Apollo and flayed alive, traces in the pavonazzetto, 'the thin pink veins [...] which evince / a body, stripped of its skin'. The poem concludes at Marsyas's burial site, but the stench of his corpse is the stench of the vengeful and callous. The promise of Christian redemption comes under fire here, and the poem is a mode of resistance to narratives and individuals that collude in injustice:
And since it predicts redress, is dilute with
The largesse of the much better informed,
The grief of Christ is inauthentic.

This is not.

The title poem lists 'go' commands in five six-line stanzas, a simple organising structure that produces an attentive documentation of contemporary Western culture. 'Go Giants' begins with cartoonish childhood reminiscence – 'Go go gadget legs' – and ends with violent instruction – 'Go for the throat'. The go-getting imperative is a logic elsewhere destabilised in a collection that muses on our delusional attraction to the idea of advancement. Laird is attuned to a frequency that feels immediate and familiar, nudging us to notice how unthinkingly we can decode an insurance broker's invitation from a catchphrase that emphasises personal freedom. We might also notice the atomic bomb as a subject of political advertisement, a form of insurance from the perceived threat of global terrorism. All of this from the placement of two two-word commands: 'Go compare. Go nuclear.' Deft parataxis exemplifies the skill involved in composing a lively, humorous and intelligent poem entirely from instructions and platitudes. It also shows Laird's respect for, and trust in, the reader. The commands of Jesus, the priest and old spirituals sit cheek by jowl with American football chants, eco-speak, deathbed advice and capitalist cliché. We are given the chance to notice and compare the nuances of these tired imperatives and all that they reveal about our love of purposeful action.

The dull, loving intimacies of 'Talking in Kitchens' reveal Laird's knack for recording the banality and preciousness of home life, where 'we've talked ourselves out / and we feel as we feel every day of the year // like nobody knows how we feel and it's fine'. The dark, butchered sonnet, 'Spree', meanwhile, is a nursery rhyme nightmare of violent deaths that blames a nameless male Other – Death, or God – for murderous efficiency performed with smug contentment. 'The Workshop' and 'History of the Sonnet' are brilliant and timely antidotes to the explanatory tedium of creative writing classes taught, these days, by many poets, Laird among them. The last line of the latter is one slang word repeated four times. Echoing the title of a mid-nineties pop song about sex in iambic pentameter, the line fulfils the title's promise delightfully: "Sumthin' sumthin', sumthin', sumthin', sumthin'". I could have done without the quirky twenty-something's boasts of 'The Package from Latvia'. At times, too, there is an adolescent rage about the volume's attempts to 'backslide / on god and spurn the tribe and go outside / and slam the door behind me, hard' and its angry direct address to God. This is self-consciously Psalmic, of course – the soundtrack to the last poem is '*Miserere mei, Deus* // on repeat' – but such demonstrations of rejection seem occasionally more insistent than they might need to be.

'Progress', the long poem with which *Go Giants* concludes, is ambitious, though I'm not sure that all of the title headings taken from Bunyan's *Pilgrim's Progress* work to structure and enhance its reminiscences and reflections as fruitfully as they might. Some of these parenthetical subtitles interrupt sentences, disrupting the teleological progress of the Christian journey effectively enough. But some of the connections between the episodes indicated and the sections of the poem seem rather tangential. Laird uses the allegorical text to treat Irish history and to structure much more personal reflections, but I found myself wanting a more sustained engagement with the meaning and value of Bunyan's text and its legacies in Protestant Ulster. I should issue the disclaimer, though, that my knowledge of *Pilgrim's Progress* comes from an abridged illustrated edition awarded to me as child as a prize for memory verse recitation. This kind of religious culture is also a crucial part of the volume's landscape. In the 'Mr Enmity' section of 'Progress', 'a Church of Ireland choirboy trudging home' comes to understand how enemies are made in tit-for-tat scrapes with a Catholic schoolboy. All too conscious of walking the well-trodden territory of 'Troubles poetry' and its reception, Laird bemoans 'The monotony of always being on a side!' while showing that the sectarianism that leads to a teenage boy splitting a lip, being spat on and feeling fear must nonetheless be detailed if any 'progress' is to be made.

The Cookstown meatplant setting owes something of its atmosphere to Patrick McCabe's *The Butcher Boy*, but the imagery and phrasing draw more directly from the black, white and blood-red palette of Heaney's *The Spirit Level*: 'the boiler suits were dyed bright red / so you'd hardly notice the splatters of blood'. As well as flecks of blood, and a meditation on voyeurism and perspective, the parabolic quality of some of Laird's utterances is also indebted to Heaney: 'Not hard to get blood / from a stone if it's smashed in someone's face.' If Laird is rather wearied by the bullshit of contemporary politics and the public relations efforts that accompany it, there is a counteracting verve in the language he uses to detail this atmosphere. The speaker of 'Observance' tells us, 'I watched the war on drugs / or drunk'. Like the line break, the poem wedges open new meanings in the reception of familiar speech, prompting a reflection on the impossible political slogan, the entertainment value of twenty-four hour news coverage on every available screen and the hypocrisy involved in choosing the targets of a war. The stasis and contained stench of current political and military manoeuvres is brilliantly conveyed in its final image: 'the hot soft ouroboros / of dogshit wrapped in plastic'.

'Avi' tells of a real-life employee of the *Letters to God* department of the Israeli postal service charged with the task of reading 'correspondence that can neither be delivered / nor returned satisfactorily to the sender' before dispatching the letters to the Western Wall. The penultimate stanza is a list of nineteen apostrophes that reveal a history of political and religious strife: 'O Rabi Jesus, His Reverence, The High Priest, [...] Klagemauer, Israel, King David, Jerusalem'. The Hallmark greetings card appearance of the centrally justified stanzas gently foregrounds the sentimentality of the epistolary endeavour. But the poem is also sensitive and sympathetic to those letter-writers who 'want to be happy, forgiven or healed'. Along with the Big Sweep hopefuls, 'A sufferer / in stage four doesn't want her son to be alone', 'Condolence' provides a tender portrait of another letter-writing mother, and a memorable image of bereavement. It is this balance of scepticism and empathy that makes *Go Giants* so memorable a volume. Laird has a quiet but passionate determination to make language matter in a context where it seems that it shouldn't or can't. There may be no progress, but there is movement, action, colour, and sound in poems redirecting our attention to our 'miraculous flesh'.

Drysalter is Michael Symmons Roberts's sixth collection of poetry, made up of 150 poems of 15 lines. The title refers to a dealer in drugs, chemicals, powders and cures, as well as to the writer of the Psalms. The structure and ambition of the collection is a brave undertaking but it doesn't pay off. The collection has been praised for its meditation on transcendence but, put simply, you can't have transcendence until you've described the earth worth transcending. There is an annoying lack of specificity about the landscapes and histories depicted in *Drysalter*. While *Go Giants* has heart, *Drysalter* reads like poetry without a pulse. As the titles alone suggest, the impulse of the former is energetic celebration and critique; the latter, preservation of the status quo. The first poem, 'World into Fragments' describes 'a world more fragile than we thought'. As the ice caps melt, floods rise, economies crash and privacies are compromised, one wonders why any reader would doubt the fragility of the world and our hold on things. There is an obviousness to statements like this that wearies me. I felt the same way about 'There is no way to the soul / but through the body' ('Hymn to November') and the metaphor of 'History as layers of paint, sedimentary' ('Discoverers'). Imagining the human body placed into a glass case of formaldehyde, 'In Cutaway' spells out its intended meaning: 'my absence / and my presence held in stasis'. Symmons Roberts underestimates his reader by not trusting them to interpret his images. This is frustrating, particularly when coupled with his attempt to provide meta-perspective – to deal with soul and body as concepts, without describing their texture and tang, their colours and contours.

The volume concludes by overturning its fragile beginnings and restoring order to the briefly glimpsed chaos. The final poem, 'Fragments into World' declares 'a recapitulation of the world we knew'. *Drysalter* ends by celebrating resolution, harmony and unification. We are commanded to 'watch / as windows heal and pull together, towers // palaces, museums [...] form and seal'. The conservatism in the circularity of the volume's construction makes the endeavour of reading these 150 poems seem like something of a fait accompli. Symmons Roberts wants to 'give thanks for the tangible and visible', but despite the speaker's insistence, in 'Hymn to November', 'I keep myself grounded', there is very little to root us in a particular place and time. Some critics love *Drysalter* for precisely that reason, praising its meditation on grace and its hymnal and Psalm-like forms for making pseudo-religious meanings available in a (post-)secular time. For me, though, Symmons Roberts' attempt to use the old adages doesn't feel new enough to hold my attention. He shows that this is a self-conscious undertaking in 'Night Train': 'one idea, say, *life as journey*'. From my view, this is too close to cliché to be called new. When he writes of the Psalmist's bedsheet, 'streaked with jizz, sweat, grime', Symmons Roberts demonstrates his capacity for perceptive specificity in well-chosen words ('streaked' a half rhyme with 'grief'). In 'String Theory', simple premises unravel into a thoughtful fantasy of an abandoned finance house that was

stripped bare, floor-by-floor when

bets went sour, and work-stations were lost
to crates and sacks, bailiffs packed up chairs,
screens blanked, water-coolers calcified.

'The Road Retaken' describes an atmosphere indebted to Cormac McCarthy's novel in reverse, as someone walks backwards into the desert. The weird direction and process of removing 'gadgets and accoutrements, / then garments' is compelling, and the landscape depicted in the pairs of lines is rendered in attentive detail. But the final line's imperative tense commands irritate by swapping observation for authorial control: 'Turn round. Drop to all fours. Now run.' There is much too much of the imperative tense for my liking in *Drysalter*. 'Necessary and Sufficient Causes' is a strangely perverse parable that uses rhyme to its advantage. In poems like this,

Symmons Roberts trusts the reader enough to let such strangeness linger without conceptual explanation. But getting through these 150 fifteen-line poems felt too much like struggling under deadweight. The conceptual ideas behind *Drysalter* are strong and the poems are technically coherent and controlled. Sadly, though, most of them make me feel nothing. Nothing seems at stake. Laird risks looking vulnerable by showing versions of himself as traumatised child, masturbating teen, jittery plainsong-listener and city-dwelling lover. Symmons Roberts doesn't risk anything that honest. Like salt, his poems preserve what exists without questioning too much the whys and wherefores of the business of being alive. I'm inclined to put my faith in Laird. ♦

GAIL McCONNELL

'Caught up in all the Catchings of the eye'

Gerald Dawe, *Selected Poems*, Gallery, £10.75
Andrew Jamison, *Happy Hour*, Gallery, £10.50

When asked in an interview with Culture Northern Ireland which line of his own poetry he is most proud of, Gerald Dawe cited the final couplet of 'The Pleasure Boats': '*So, tell me, what good was done, / what war was won?*' Originally published in Points West, the poem is reprinted in Dawe's *Selected Poems*, recently released by Gallery Books. The poet's choice is revealing. These lines could serve as epigraph or coda to this selection, crystalizing as they do Dawe's enduring preoccupation with the shifting socio-political climate in his native Northern Ireland, and his writerly engagement with, as he puts it in 'Morning Start', 'a smattering of words'.

Representing three decades of work, *Selected Poems* brings together poems from Dawe's first collection, *Sheltering Places*, published by Blackstaff Press in 1978, with selections from *The Lundys Letter* (1985) through to *Points West* (2008). As the acknowledgements indicate, some titles have been changed, and occasional revisions have been introduced, but for the most part *Selected Poems* retains all the hallmarks of Dawe's distinctive voice and his characteristically haunting evocations of specific places and times. Unlike the majority of 'selecteds', this one is not interrupted by headings signposting the titles and dates of the original collections. While the seventy one poems presented here are arranged in chronological order, the achievement of Dawe's *Selected* is that it reads as an integrated, intellectually and emotionally engaging narrative movement, and so stands as a collection in its own right. At the same time, it proffers an effectively orchestrated arc through Dawe's *oeuvre* to date.

Appropriately, the book opens with the title poem from *Sheltering Places*. Composed a decade into the Troubles, and indicative of the profound impact the civil strife would have on a generation of Northern Irish poets, this is a fitting lead-in to a run of early poems addressing 'the Black North'. The deft conflation of a natural electric storm and

[REVIEWS]

the encroaching sectarian violence in the province culminates in the
poem's understated closing stanza:

> The storm is reaching
> home territory, stretching
> over the hills down
> into our sheltering places.

The placement of 'Names' immediately afterward signals what
would become a consistent theme in Dawe's work: the tension
between the need to escape from those 'sheltering places' and the
sense of cultural identity embedded both in location and in the
language attaching to self and others. 'I've been here having thought
/ nowhere else was possible', Dawe writes. Choosing 'the exile's way'
is, of course, no guarantee of forgetting. The poem's assertion that
on departure 'You need never recall / the other names' is ironic, and
inevitably contradicted. The ensuing sequence ('Memory', 'Secrets',
'Resistances', 'Atlantic Circle') attests to the indelible shaping
influence of Northern Ireland on Dawe's 'soul-making'. At home on
a 'shrinking island', the speaker in these early pieces finds himself
'coming of age in a sparse / attic overlooking the sluggish tide', heir to
a people 'tight-lipped about God- / knows-what secrets.' Apart yet a
part ('I'm merely visiting and able / to leave well enough alone'), in his
lonely derive he cuts a figure reminiscent of Stephen Dedalus:

> I keep the head down
> and mouth shut and walk about
> with an independent air,
> imagining all their neat homes,
> our mutual incomprehension.

Those dark and tense lyrics segue into the more tranquil tones and
pastoral imagery of poems which mark a geographic transition from the
North to the West of Ireland, principally Galway, and from outsiderish
isolation to the community of marriage, the birth of a daughter, the
'pips and squeaks of central heating', a gathering of 'family robins'.
There are moments here of romantic and domestic intimacy ('Spoils
of Love', 'Solstice', 'Three Sisters') and of playful acknowledgement
of literary exemplars ('To James Joyce' – 'I tip my hat as you pass
by, / a preoccupied man in shabby gutties'). It is a measure of Dawe's
realism, however, that even such lucent moments are shot through

with a keen awareness of underlying dangers and instability. Witness the wire- and rat-consuming pike in 'A Story', the 'sirens on the rocks' of 'The Messages' or in 'Straws in the Wind' the forces which run counter to the speaker's benevolent prayer for his daughter: 'I think I hear night-things bombard / our fragile peace: straws in the wind, / a fugitive dog sniffing the back steps.' Like the man waiting on the train platform in 'Heart of Hearts', Dawe's personae 'look intently / at each passerby because he never knows'. If such looking risks the stuff of madness, it is also what ignites the curiosity and attentiveness that power creativity.

While Dawe's poems vibrantly realize the tangible, physical world we inhabit, they are also finely tuned to places and people that have been lost or forgotten, yet may exist in flashes of dream, intuition or heightened perception. In its shift from the present moment back through layers of personal past, 'Autobiography' pans the poet's life for salient moments, bringing deep memories to surface light. At the same time, it questions conventional understandings of autobiography, revealing how fragmented and provisional notions of self and history actually are. Rummaging through memory and dream, the speaker confesses, 'What this means I cannot say'; having dug deep into his own psyche, he is left asking, 'Are you, am I, / treading upon some loose and complicated path // *of dead and living*, figures etched in the night?'

Akin to 'In Ron's Place', 'Autobiography' is a pivotal poem in terms of style and subject, expressing as it does the need to throw light on the inner reaches of self and nation. Positioned at the centre of the selection, it marks a turning point in Dawe's life and writing. Although the commitment to precise and emotive evocations of Dublin, Belfast, Derry is maintained ('The Morning Train', 'Human Wishes', 'Midsummer Report', 'The Interface', 'Laughter and Forgetting', 'Distraction', 'Snap'), from here on the poems open out to an engagement with, and indeed a psychogeographic excavation of, lives and locations beyond Ireland. Travel east into European heartlands is represented by 'Refugees', 'The Minos Hotel', 'Quartz', 'Kristalnacht, 1938', 'The Old Jewish Cemetery, Lodz', 'Text Messages', 'Lake Geneva', while 'The Moon-viewing Room' recalls a moment of stillness in a temple in Kyoto. There is across these poems a pervasive sense of liberation into a larger world of diverse landscapes, languages and identities, of historical happenings and literary traces. Dawe's immersion in the layers of history that blanket continental Europe is indicated by the epigraph from F. Scott Fitzgerald which heads up 'The Minos Hotel': *'One is in a country that is no longer here and not quite there'*. In this sequence, set on the shores of the Mediterranean, Germans and Greeks rub shoulders with French and English tourists, while the shades of Picasso, Modigliani, Eliot and Magritte cause the speaker to ask, 'What year is this? What century?' That slippage in space and time allows the poet to drink in the orderly richesse of Lake Geneva – 'The Alps at my fingertips, / the lake a dream' – while refusing to turn a deaf ear to 'The SS...polishing their boots // in the rooms overhead' or, in 'Refugees', 'Deep down in the swimming pool / a wasted army call[ing] for air and food and shelter'.

This turn to the east is complemented by selections from Dawe's most recent collection, *Points West*, in which he records with delicacy, attentiveness and a clear-sighted honesty the imprint of New World encounters. 'Points West' itself reads as a Whitmanesque catalogue of sights and sounds in an East Coast town: there are 'a dozen streets of little houses', wind chimes and a 'terrace overlooking a splendid sea', 'the uplit swimming pool', 'the first train haring off to points west'. But here as elsewhere, Dawe is not taken in by surface attractions. North America may be new and unusual, but it too has its dark underbelly: stowaways in airless container ships, the stings of tree wasps and mosquitos. A comparable set of impressions is recorded in the three sections from 'On Mill Street': there is the lure of 'exotic' mammal names like muskrat, possum and coyote, but also the unsettling presence of 'little creatures / nestling down in the basement' and the ghostly laughter of slaves from beyond the graveyards of the South's old guard.

While these excursions to distant locales clearly bring an enlivening breadth and difference to Dawe's poems, what is highlighted across the carefully designed trajectory of *Selected Poems* is the way in which these sojourns have impacted on how the poet sees and writes his home territories. If time and distance alienate, they can also clarify and sharpen understanding, and this renewed perspective is readily apparent in Dawe's more recent poems about Northern Ireland. To return to 'The Pleasure Boats', with its urge to the reader to 'close the door' on the past and head out into 'broad daylight, fresh air' juxtaposed against the image of day trippers in their pleasure boats returning to a harbor where 'all the changes' rival 'what hasn't changed', it would seem that the answer to this poem's rhetorical question, ('*So, tell me, what good was done, / what war was won?*') is a flat 'none'. However if we read 'The Pleasure Boats' in the light of the penultimate 'Argentina', it is possible to hear an alternative response. In one of the most precisely realized and strategically placed poems in the book:

> A turtle, one-hundred-years-old,
> is released into the Atlantic,
> a tracking device strapped to its back.

It is not difficult to see in this image of the turtle with its homing instinct on course for Argentina that of the returning pleasure boats, a correlative for the poet's drive to make poetry that ranges widely yet is deeply connected to the sheltering places of home. For Dawe the struggle to impose shape and form on language is bound up with his efforts as a poet to record and make sense of Northern Ireland's painful and protracted struggle towards social and political reconciliation. Given the caliber of those poems collected together in this volume, it is clear that for Dawe the battle for poetic virtuosity has been won, and genuine good done.

Whereas *Selected Poems* stands as a culmination of Dawe's work to date, Andrew Jamison's *Happy Hour* is a setting out. Jamison is a vibrant new voice on the Irish poetry scene, and already he has earned a number of literary distinctions: the Templar Pamphlet Award (2011), UK representative at the 2011 International Biennale of Young Artists in Rome, the Arts Council of Northern Ireland's New York Residency (2011) and the ACES Award (2012). *Happy Hour*, published by Gallery, is his first full collection and adds to these achievements a debut which boasts both formal dexterity and an engagingly idiosyncratic way of looking at the world.

Jamison was born and raised in County Down, and like the post-Heaney poets who are clearly his exemplars (there are traces here, sometimes too overt, of Paul Muldoon, Ciaran Carson, Alan Gillis) many of his poems engage with the urban and pastoral geographies of home places. The naming of numerous local and more exotic locations, from Crossgar and Carryduff to Brooklyn and Leeds, lend the collection a Joycean specificity and contribute to a verbal mapping of worlds that are at once intensely present yet already vanishing. A plethora of references to brand names, store franchises, pubs and cinemas are interspersed with meditations on the passing of seasons, lost loves and the 'a tick a tick, a tock a tock' of 'the clock on the wall' to point up a central preoccupation, namely the transience and impermanence of everything. The first poem's opening image of 'An unstubbed cigarette butt' is equivalent to 'the water neither flowing / nor still' in the final poem, 'River Run', and like the title of the collection together they foreground how fleeting life's joys are and how futile, but also how poignant and noble and humorous, our efforts to fix and hold them.

There is, accordingly, a deep and genuine sense of nostalgia running through Jamison's work, but it is generally tempered by a comic-ironic awareness of the pitfalls of self-indulgent sentimentality. As he writes in 'This Whole Place', a moving but humorous evocation of the pathos of the human condition, 'There is nostalgia deep in the very bolts / of these steel seats outside the Europa bus station...There is disappointment deep / in the mayonnaise of my chicken sandwich'. And while he is well able to conjure the childhood adventure of going to the pictures in the Curzon cinema – 'each aisle a dotted runway strip / as seats are taken, lights dimmed, minds blown' – he is careful to objectify that look back by making it an example of just how partial and provisional our subjective perceptions of place and time actually are:

> And yet the building seemed
> so small, so humble from without
> as if itself some sort of optical illusion,
> some special effect, a trick of the eye
> that got us every time.

The nostalgia, disappointment, and melancholy which, as Jamison recognizes, are the natural responses to so much evanescence, are likewise warded off by a MacNeiceian reveling in the delight of things being rich and various. This is a poetry which takes huge linguistic delight in the music and colour of the world in the present moment. Clearly a connoisseur of contemporary music (there are a number of poems here which take their cue from listening to bands including Ash, Kings of Convenience and Them), Jamison's facility for the sound effects of assonance, consonance, onomatopoeia, internal rhyme and, on occasion, regular rhythm and rhyme is sophisticated and energized, and in itself proves a nourishing counter to life's sweet but swift passage. The opening poem in the collection, 'The Bus to Belfast', is indicative of Jamison's skill in shaping soundscapes that echo the sense they carry:

> The tenner I tender will elicit an epic *tut*
> from the part-time bodybuilder driver,
> raising the plucked eyebrows on his sunbed-seared mug.

That hyper-awareness of poetry's music, and of its intrinsic connection to meaning, is the subject of 'Listening to Them', in which the speaker, trying to mimic Van's 'Baby Please Don't go' on his 'Epiphone acoustic', admits, 'I think over each single, solitary lyric'. The implication that the musician/poet thinks above and beyond, and yet at the same time through, every word and line is part of an emergent *ars poetica* also articulated in 'Chancer', a humorous self-portrait replete with wordplay at the close of which the poet confesses: 'I, in my own way, am a gambling man: / I'm putting pen to paper, here and now, / and hoping to God the going is good.'

Jamison's linguistic playfulness is as much a bulwark against the vicissitudes of time as a source of artistic pleasure. It is also an aural register of the verbal and visual flotsam and jetsam that wash through our existence, a music that finds its counterpart in the many images of movement which weave through the poems in *Happy Hour*. On the one hand, the condition of motion is shown to be an end in itself, a pleasurable retreat from action and demand, yet paradoxically it is also figured as an immersion in the unstoppable flow of time and its fleeting forms. The anticipated bus ride from Crossgar to Belfast is imagined as both a still moment and a cross-country dash:

A flash of sun
will flare first, then flicker for a while through my eyes
as we hurtle past Pizza Hut, Winemark, then the Spar.
We shuffle by Forestside. Nothing will have changed.

Jamison is a poet invested in 'meandering', whether, as in the poem bearing that title, through memories of places and people or, as he does in some of the longer and arguably most accomplished pieces in the collection, though the loose, long-lined forms he works in 'Transatlantic', 'Thinking about the Point of Things' and the single-sentence 'New Year in Belfast'. These are poems that operate via accumulation and association, gaining momentum as they go. In the case of 'Thinking about the Point of Things', the line of sight moves from the widescreen sky-vista of a plane descending into Belfast city airport, through the election-poster festooned streets of the speaker's home town and into his mother's kitchen, his father's garden, where tight focus on a solo robin, 'skitter[ing] through the leylandii...makes me see an order in the world, a system, / and think it's not so bad, it's not all doom and gloom.'

That kind of optimism, although inflected with a realistic acknowledgment of humanity's sufferings and shortcomings, remains the dominant note in *Happy Hour*. Akin to Dawe, Jamison records the darker aspects of his own 'sheltering places' but as a younger poet, one brought up not in the midst but rather in the wake of the Troubles, he is able to make greater light of this 'province of 'politics'': 'the same old same old from the same old-timers / while buccaneery young bucks bear the look of the duped'. And while a clutch of poems about time spent in London, Yorkshire and New York City, like those 'after' the Spanish poet Jorge Guillen ('Death's Door'), the Brazilian Manuel Bandeira ('The Early Hours') and Pablo Neruda ('Killyleagh Road at Night in Snow'), attest to the creative outcomes of travel and of engaging with a range of languages and cultures, those other spaces and voices are essentially of a piece with Jamison's take on Northern Ireland. In the big picture, he implies, each of us is 'eating alone in an empty diner', subject in our isolation to the inevitability of time's arrow. Yet we are all also, like the swirling birds imaged in 'The Starlings', surely the most exquisite poem in this promising collection, 'beautiful obliterations of the commonplace'.

KATHLEEN McCRACKEN

Damaged Individuals

Hannah Lowe, *Chick*, Bloodaxe, £8.95
Claire Pollard: *Ovid's Heroines*, Bloodaxe, £9.95

Chick is Hannah Lowe's first full-length collection, its title being her late father's nickname. The book is an emotionally raw and clear-eyed examination of the poet's relationship with a deeply complicated character, a mix of angry and dignified elegy and celebration both for him and for the victims of life in inner-city London in the late 20th century. The book's strategy of moving non-chronologically between accounts of her father, her friends and her own life in the present effectively envelops the reader in the poet's attempts to make sense of her father's life and the social circumstances and individual impulses that conditioned it. That Lowe manages to keep these volatile elements in balance – in the sense of reserving judgement and maintaining narrative tension – is a big part of what makes *Chick* such an absorbing, engaging work.

The book confronts the reader with close-up portrayals of hungry, angry, damaged individuals, and Lowe's numerous love poems are hard-earned moments of sanctuary, though even these are marked by loneliness and the encroaching fear of social condemnation. The poem 'Sausages' is as much about the resistance to her parents' relationship as the relationship itself, the relative drabness of the neighbours' lives ('mince and cabbage') and their own mutual emotional security located evocatively in the act of preparing food. This is a subtly recurring theme, as the book's brief, contingently affirmative moments are consistently found in the sensuality of eating; 'Artisan du Chocolat, Borough Market' ('hands round our mugs as we lull / our poor hearts with sweetness and sugar'), 'Antonio, in the Coffee Shop' ('how many times must you have wiped / an errant splotch of cream or buttermilk / or icing from that perfect chin, those lips?'), 'Poem with a Plaintain in it' and 'A Man Can Cook' all find a stay against the book's violence, uprootedness and uncertainty.

Violence is in the bedrock of the story, both within and without the family unit, as succinctly sketched in the short poem 'Say': 'Say that your mother took in a lodger,' and after a spell of calm, 'Say he sometimes cooked dinner [...] your mother was plumper and happier', 'and all of a sudden the lodger was standing / and punching your brother, and after / you cried in your bedroom for hours. / And say that the lodger / was really your father, no, say.' Late in the book, the reader is aware of the game from the off, there is no twist, the poem bitterly and inevitably walks the reader through the logic of a home life it has taken an entire book to rationalise.

And this, I think, is the point the book intends: although there is ample reason to dislike Chick the character, he is carefully contextualised (though not *excused*). *Chick* never finally settles on a simple, static judgement, and in its depiction of *the father*'s last days (finding a direct ancestor in Sharon Old's The Father, particularly in 'Six Days in March', 'You want to piss // and so I carry you, / the weightless body folded in my arms.') vocalises the book's central question, 'What's a life made of?' The poem is inconclusive, 'Fifteen pounds...a notebook... one photograph...?', but the book provides its own answer. Chick is a compelling, harsh collection of poems.

Clare Pollard's translation of Ovid's *Heroines* is presented explicitly as an academic endeavour, the author's introduction locating the book both in its critical context and in the author's experience as a reader. Although a valuable and enlightening initiation to what has been carelessly (and often maliciously) overlooked as a major work and an imaginative innovation, the details of the trip that occasioned the writing (weddings in Rome and Santorini) give the impression that *Ovid's Heroines* is intended as a light holiday read. The poems have inherent dramatic potential, and the stated goal of rescuing them from obscurity and asserting the value of decentralised perspectives on myth (a compelling ongoing discussion, cf. Atwood's *Penelopiad*) is detrimentally framed. Still, the translations themselves are reasonably engaging, and are an accessible entry point for Ovid's lesser-known work.

Where the translation stumbles is in the brave attempt to update some of the tone and idiom, to emphasise the contemporary concerns of the cast of Heroines. In the most notable misstep, 'Deinira to Hercules', the introduction's conception of Deinira as 'a kind of classical WAG' is rendered in the text as faux-tabloid headlines: '*Poison Shirt Shock: Demands for Deinira's Death*'. The original awkward dramatization of Deinira continuing to write to her husband after learning of his death is compounded by the translations' lurch in tone. Though the conventions of the original are partly to blame, the book's uneven register, vacillating between contemporary and classical, give *Ovid's Heroines* the feel of an early draft.

Formally, Pollard wisely avoids reproducing Ovid's rhyming couplets; it is to the detriment of the work that little other formal control stands in its place, as several sections drag and lack dramatic shape, Ovid's occasional windiness is given insufficient formal support. It's notable that the sections rendered in rhythmically flexible quatrains (or section XIII, a piece split into smaller fragments), keep an energetic pace and better retain their dramatic tension. The closing piece, in which Ovid essentially ventriloquises his feelings through an invented Sappho, also feels the benefits of relaxed imaginative freedom in Pollard's version.

The stories themselves accumulate a genuinely moving sense of entrapment as a series of women – most of them powerful within their own communities, some supernaturally so – are reduced to passive sufferers, often suicidal, often abandoned to their fate. Although, as Pollard points out, Ovid is no proto-feminist, the text nevertheless demonstrates these women's limited roles in the founding myths of a civilisation, myths with deep roots in contemporary culture. It is tempting to wonder what *Heroines* might have been with more license to roam from the original text, or even to tell its own versions; as is, Ovid's *Heroines* is a worthy piece somewhat hamstrung by tonal and formal inconsistencies.

DAVE COATES

Poetry of Departures

Richard Murphy, *The Pleasure Ground: Poems 1952-2012*, Bloodaxe, £12.

In *Seven Winters* (1942) Elizabeth Bowen recorded the childhood confusion that

> made me take the words "Ireland" and "island" to be synonymous. Thus, all other countries quite surrounded by water took (it appeared) their generic name from ours. It seemed fine to live in a country that was a prototype. England, for instance, was "an ireland" (or, a sub-Ireland) - an imitation. Then I learned that England was not even "an Ireland", having failed to detach herself from the flanks of Scotland and Wales. Vaguely, as a Unionist child, I conceived that our politeness to English must be a form of pity.

At first glance, Richard Murphy would seem likely to share Elizabeth Bowen's confusion. He comes, after all, from a similar Anglo-Irish background and the word 'island' rings through his poetry: from the title poem of his first full collection *Sailing to an Island* (1963) to 1974's *High Island* both the word and references to specific instances of islands recur. However, 'Sailing to an Island' makes clear from the start that Ireland is by no means his prototype island, but rather only one among many. Ireland is being left behind as the poem opens, and arrival at Clare, 'our chosen island' (*The Pleasure Ground*, 19), is frustrated by sea, storm and the state of the boat. The passengers are lucky and glad to find safe harbour in Inishbofin, though as the last stanzas show, the speaker's passage through a night of drinking is just as storm-tossed as his voyage. All in all the poem signals a turning away from Ireland as a whole, unnamed in this poem and named only rarely in the poetry through which the names of western isles, Mediterranean islands and littorals, and Ceylon/Sri Lanka run. If an island name underwrites all of this it is as likely to be the 'strong brand name' of 'Serendip' as 'Ireland' ('Sri Lanka', *TPG*, 233) as Murphy's poetry restlessly, even relentlessly, moves with little motivation from one place to another.

In our current sense of the chronology of contemporary poetry, Richard Murphy belongs to that awkward betwixt and between generation which also includes Thomas Kinsella and John Montague. They were writers for whom Joyce (via Patrick Kavanagh) arguably provided more of a model and a challenge than did Yeats, and who had the chance, before the outbreak of the Troubles, to speak of 'bygone spleen', as Murphy did in *The Battle of Aughrim* ('Orange March', *TPG*, 63). For a time, at least, objective attention might be paid to the actualities of a present life more concerned with work and relationships than with history. *The Pleasure Ground* (replacing the *Collected Poems* of 2000) bears this out; here are the poems, for which Murphy is well-known, of boat-building and sailing, the poems of house building and furniture making. As 'Bookcase for *The Oxford English Dictionary*' (TPG, 162) makes clear these activities are always located within relationships and so, as well as equating to the construction of poems, they provide the poems with their social world.

Murphy's poems are certainly well-constructed and this volume has a heft to it which is in part made up of about 40 pages of notes, often adapted from *The Kick: A Memoir* (2002), on the 'provenance' of various poems (as well as Bernard O'Donoghue's characteristically astute essay on 'Pat Cloherty's Version of *The Maisie*'). The first of these – 'Author's note on the provenance of "Sailing to an Island"' – tells us that 'the poem I had drafted at Rosroe [in 1952], revised and revised, emerged in 1963 as the final version... '. That Murphy was already trying to write 'an obscurely mythological mini-epic called "Voyage to an Island"' (TPG, 245) before this gives the poem an even longer gestation. With the appearance of *The Kick* in 2002 and 'A River of Notebooks' here, we are now familiar with Murphy's lifelong habit of keeping notebooks and 'fish[ing] for poems' (TPG, 236) in them. This gives a consistency to the voice that we hear throughout his work, but it also sets up what is ultimately a jarring contrast between that consistency and his subject matter. The autobiographical introduction, 'The Pleasure Ground', which owes much to an article from *The Listener* in 1963, significantly tells us that 'Neither he [Murphy's father] not his Murphy forbears [sic] had ever owned a house or an acre of land' (TPG, 13). Just how far back those forebears might go is left deliberately unclear: we know from other places that 'forbears' fought on both sides at *the Battle of Aughrim*, and the possibility that this son of Empire – his father 'a senior civil servant in the crown colony of Ceylon' – derives from men of no property is real. The young Murphy and his brother occupy, temporarily, *the Pleasure Ground* 'a seedy paradise of impoverished Anglo-Irish pride' (PG, 13) Not surprisingly, implicit and explicit variations on the question 'Who owns the land?' run through The Battle of Aughrim, and Murphy's poetry is frequently concerned with this as both an historical and a contemporary question:

> With what shall I buy
> From time's auctioneers
> This old property
> Before it disappears? ('Auction', TPG, 27)

It may be an exaggeration to put it this strongly, but this is a poetry of acquisitions; boats, houses, an island, a goat ('Care', TPG, 148-9) are all bought. In turn, much descriptive effort goes into the accounts of renovation and renewal of boats and buildings. These renewals are seen as valid in their own right and valorised further through juxtaposition. In 'Slate' the speaker takes pride in paving his 'garden path / With slate St Colman nailed on lath' and this seems more fitting than the behaviour of his 'kinsman' in the following poem, 'Inheritance', who has 'broadened his pigsty roof' with 'Slate he stripped from a Church of Ireland steeple' (TPG, 66-7). Reading through the whole collection, however, raises the unsettling question of what happens to these various properties – we know that the goat in 'Care' dies, her instincts tamed – but as each new project emerges in the poetry we are left wondering whether the previous ones are simply now the 'refuse of time' on which poetry feeds ('A River of Notebooks', TPG, 236). Ruin seems to pile up in Murphy's wake. It's not just Ireland that is being left behind throughout this poetry, but much else into which various energies have been poured. The note of abstention, introduced serendipitously by the typo 'forbear', reinforces the question as to whether anything is ever fully engaged. His fine elegy for his maternal grandmother 'The Woman of the House' (TPG, 29-32) – its title ironically gesturing towards the impossible distance between her and the idea of the *bean an tí* – is framed by the opposition between 'the guest room' in which he is born and 'the family earth' in which she is buried. Murphy, going beyond the idea that the Anglo-Irish live in their hyphen, writes a poetry ultimately of departures. The visitors of

'Battle Hill Revisited' may 'try to imagine / Exactly what took place and what it could mean' but do not miss their 'plane for France' (TPG, 100). Murphy writes a poetry which tries to imagine the same things but 'the house I've left' ('Niches', TPG, 155) is in the end his most important location. By this token the 50 sonnets of *The Price of Stone* are 50 farewells to places that will always inevitably be left.

If Murphy's restless energy is to be admired – though one could wish that it would more often find an equivalent spontaneity in the poetry – this worrying question of what remains in its aftermath is provoked by the sheer scope of this volume which has something altogether too monumental about it. It generates an overpowering sense of disconnection and Murphy's work might be better served by a *Selected* in which the rare but wonderful moments of connectedness would have more space. 'Seals at High Island', for example, is a great poem about the disconnections of love and sex, and the distance between the human and the animal. However, just as the poem identifies disconnections and distances and, indeed, their necessity, it establishes, through its other subject – the erotics of voice and language, here present as rhyme and alliteration – a form of connection which defies such separation:

> But I must remember
> How far their feelings are from mine marooned.
> If there are tears at this holy ceremony
> Theirs are caused by brine and mine by breeze. (*TPG*, 143-4)

EAMONN HUGHES

'The debt all losses owe to Sentiment'

Connor O'Callaghan, *The Sun King*, Gallery, 2013, £10.50
Leanne O'Sullivan, *The Mining Road*, Bloodaxe, 2013, £8.95

During his third building campaign of the Palace of Versailles, the other Sun King, Louis XIV, commissioned the construction of a hall of mirrors as a gesture of his opulence and preference for finery, an act of vanity rather than introspection. Dan Chiasson, writing for Poetry Magazine has already noted of O'Callaghan's previous collection *Fiction* (Gallery, 2005) its "house-of-mirrors deceits and self-deceits of estranged lovers", and some of these concerns haunt this, his fourth collection. It is a collection of various considerations that include the hubristic exuberance of Celtic Tiger Ireland, technology's ubiquity and ever pressing encroachment on language – as the internet becomes a pastoral landscape of its own.

The Sun King opens with 'Lordship', a poem far-reaching in its exposition – the two prongs of its title take us from the rural townland in Louth to London via Belfast through destablising shifts of tone and voice: a writer discussing his narrator, a lover's recollection of romantic *events* mediated through an anaphoric 'Once'. O'Callaghan has said himself that in this book he's "tried to write about sex, money and the internet", and it seems to me this opening poem is emblematic of the design and ambit of the collection at large. Reflections on debt and economic precariousness are glanced at throughout the collection; "real estate signs were popping along the coast / like crocus bulbs come late to flowering" in the opening poem. Financial insecurity shows up often by way of analogy – 'Sospeso' refers to the charitable act of buying in a café a 'suspended' coffee that a more needy person might claim; in 'Peace', he wants a "term in currency" for "the debt all losses owe to sentiment / for loss that wakes in happiness; a grief- / nostalgia some Germanic compound coins / and we don't share."
The invective 'Tiger Redux' most explicitly confronts the "waves and boom" years of the Irish economy to the metre of Blake's 'The Tyger', setting the incomplete catalectic line against the Republic's capitulation to the recession after the sing-song "jouissance" of its rise:

Magic back designer shakes,
gold-soaked morning-after flakes,
fibre optics, soft-top wheels,
tax incentive movie stills,

Xerox plants like pleasure domes,
sushi bars, the second homes,
investment apts in Budapest,
light rail lanes, the glitz, the rest.

Elsewhere, we have a number of poems addressing the matter of poetry in translation, and the wider act of translating one thing into another – for example, when "That truck and blossoms story gets longer, / hokier, with each retelling." ('Swell') The poem 'Translation' itself invites the reader to "Imagine you are this poem / moments before it is translated". Heaney supposed that "Most poems in translation are affairs" and that quip sits nicely beside O'Callaghan's translation (it's closer in comparative meaning and shape than to be a 'version') of Lorca's 'La Casada Infiel'. His English 'The Unfaithful Housewife' ruminates on the faithful translation or what the idea of it might be.

The central and most powerful poem for my money is 'Kingdom Come'. As a poem of estrangement and longing, its effect is realised with technical mastery. It glances both to a kingdom in disrepair, allowing its title to fall just short of *thy will be done*, certainly playing on the Lord of the opening poem. Its fifteen couplets have a presence of effacement and a dilution of stability. It's a performance of ghostly doublings of sound and many of the rhymes are appropriately slant. If the poetic line might be structured as a unit of breath, these couplets are anxious; three and four beat lines strive against each other, reaching for a sort of rhetorical balance:

Mostly I mark papers
by light run off the alternator.

Though lately I've been praying, lady,
that whatever kingdom come there is

is a street we owned a place on
where the life we meant to love

and ran screaming from mid-stream
completes itself without us

and it's evening over and over again.

Dorianne Laux has said that "a poem that does its work must stand on
the knife edge of yes and no. The last line of a poem should have both
the yes and the no in it" and this is certainly true of 'Kingdom Come',
it ends with the couplet

And I, in some shape or form,
am there as well. And you are there.

The collection is formally accomplished, playfully encompassing
concrete poems, a master class in sibilant friskiness ('In Praise of
Sprinklers') and also traditional forms such as a villanelle and sonnets
pushed in various directions – the long lines of 'The End of the Line'
not only announce their own presence by appearing landscape in the
book, but oblige the reader to acknowledge it by turning the book 90°
to read the poem.

Any talk of form or shape in this collection must address the last
poem, 'The Pearl Works'. It alludes to a 19th Century cutlery factory
in Sheffield, but also, surely, to the 14th Century alliterative poem 'The
Pearl'. It consists of 45 couplets of exactly 140 characters, starting as it
did, as a project on Twitter to write a poem for each week of the year.
It contains some of the finest images and patterns in the book. Take,
for example:

And this? The handful of coppers daylight borrows from October.
Come bright hour. Be bright. Be ours. Be extra, ecstatic, immaterial,
other.

The poem and collection builds to a marvellous chiming of assonant

'O' sounds, becoming a pearl, a sun, a circle, a wonderment. The book is an achievement of articulacy, imagination, and poignancy. In 'A Nest of Tables', the speaker "could use / a sunrise". The Sun King is its own sunrise.

Leanne O'Sullivan's third collection, *The Mining Road* roots her poems well in the Irish lyric. It is preoccupied with the landscape of provincial West Cork as well as the landscape of memory both personal and communal. These memories are tempered and accessed through the legacy of the copper mines that operated at varying degrees of productivity in Allihies. (Indeed the remoteness of this landscape might be summed up by its museum's website's boast that it's the most "inaccessible museum" in the country.) The collection though, is not inaccessible. The opening poem, 'Townland' is satisfyingly gothic, recalling a second-hand ghostly encounter with one Norah Seer, whom the speaker then finds herself pursuing:

> Old homes and a half remembered word of mouth;
> we'd prowl the lanes ourselves calling her out

The psychogeographic impulse persists throughout these poems – where nothing, certainly copper is anymore excavated, the environment is still charged and O'Sullivan inspects an often anecdotal history of those "old homes", the "roofless village" and, as one of many examples of her rich imagination, "the old stone walls / the swallows going like windborne rumours." This energetic sort of imagery finds itself against more earthy acuities of description, seeing in 'Irish Weather', "the blown char and armour from saucepans". Besides this, the intersection between memory and imagination throws up lines that feel more instinctive than perfect images – 'You Were Born at Mealtime' for instance starts:

> The empty kitchen hummed when I came home
> like a swollen river with the swelling gone.
> The place was all muscle in her absence

Many poems here are comfortable around the pentameter line, and we can see O'Sullivan's skill with "muscle" – the inverted iamb gives

the line an appropriate toughness.
The book is divided into two sections, largely arbitrarily it seems, as
there is no discernable change of mood or style between *The Road* and
The Store. Nevertheless, the four rhymed couplets of 'The Storehouse'
are elegantly plotted. "Where two pillars remember a way in", she
writes, "we will have to imagine it again". Throughout the book, we
find the poet 'imagining' a number of times. The consequence of this
is that we come to anticipate this sort of cadence; it tends to telegraph
O'Sullivan's turns so that we see 'the poem' announcing itself. The
collection presents too a number of elegies and love poems. The
"remarkable love poems", as Michael Longley has them, are rich and
charming with assurance – they seem to occupy a register of clarity
entirely their own, as in 'Antique Cabinets':

> And what would I make of such an inheritance?
> When you are gone and I am left wondering
> what should keep of love and trees and shadows,
> I imagine myself not surprised to find
> the settled world steady among your things.

One of the most intriguing genres of poem in *The Mining Road* is the
'version'. O'Sullivan includes a section from *Táin Bó Fraích*: 'Fraoch',
another love poem. The mythical character is described "straight as a
reed, carrying between his throat / and white face the red berries of
the rowan bush." Her poem 'House Lore' is *'after Michael Longley'*.
Curiously, her poem 'Argos', which rewrites Longley's poem of the
same name has no acknowledgement. 'The Border Journey' appears
to address Seamus Heaney directly. It's first section is uneven, full of
chopped, short lines, unbalanced couplets and dropped lines – it is the
only formally 'disordered' poem in the collection, so to speak: "and all
the singing / of your hands beside me / was every permanent thing".
The second of its two sections – in two mannerly sets of five lines –
is more typical of her formal preferences. This part offers another
perspective on his poem 'Electric Light', "where you stood alone / in
the darkening room and levered electric light / for the first time from
a switch on the wall."

Taken with the other versions of poems in this book, it signals

O'Sullivan as a poet who, at times, wears her influences heavily. Alongside 'Fraoch', it points perhaps to a conception of the two Northern poets inhabiting a sphere cognate with Irish myth. Either way, imagination and memory are neurologically similar processes, and it's perhaps the exploration of these two impulses that leads her to this practice of 'versioning' usually reserved for appraisals of translations and discussion of the 'literal' or 'faithful' translation. *The Mining Road* speaks to the persistence in memory, or by tangible fragments, of what is no longer present: industry, place, people. It speaks also to the instinct to recover and to be again in the light of those things. O'Sullivan's success and poignancy lies in the confidence that, in her landscape, in 'a stride of fir trees', these things have not been forgotten.

STEPHEN SEXTON

CONTRIBUTOR NOTES

GARY ALLEN has published thirteen collections of poetry. Most recently, *White Lines* (Arrowhead Press) and *Mexico* (Agenda Editions) both appeared in 2013. Gary Allen has been widely published in international magazines, including, *Ambit, Dark Horse, Edinburgh Review, Fiddlehead, Irish Pages, London Magazine, Malahat Review, Meanjin, Poetry Ireland Review, The Poetry Review, Prairie Schooner, Stand,* and *The Threepenney Review.*

EVA BOURKE is originally from Germany but has lived in Ireland most of her life. She has published six collections of poetry, most recently *piano* (2011, Dedalus Press), two comprehensive anthologies of contemporary Irish poets in German translation, as well as a collection by the German poet Elisabeth Borchers. She teaches poetry in the MfA program at NUI Galway and is a member of Aosdána. Jan Wagner was born in 1971 in Hamburg and is considered one of the best young German poets.

FRAN BREARTON is Professor of Modern Poetry at Queen's University, Belfast. Her books include *The Great War in Irish Poetry* (2000), *Reading Michael Longley* (2006), and, co-edited with Alan Gillis, *The Oxford Handbook of Modern Irish Poetry* (2012).

NIALL CAMPBELL grew up on the island of South Uist, one of the Western Isles of Scotland. He has been a recipient of an Eric Gregory Award and the Arvon-Jerwood Mentorship Scheme, and won the Poetry London Competition in 2013. His first collection, *Moontide*, is a Poetry Book Society Recommendation.

CIARAN CARSON's most recent book is *In the Light Of*, adaptations of Arthur Rimbaud's *Illuminations*; forthcoming is *From Elsewhere*, translations from Jean Follain faced by dialogues with those translations.

HARRY CLIFTON has taught in Bremen and Bordeaux universities , as well as Trinity College and University College Dublin. He was Ireland Professor of Poetry from 2010 to 2013 and his *The Holding Centre: Selected Poems 1974 - 2014* was published recently by Bloodaxe Books.

DAVE COATES grew up in Belfast and is now a first year PhD candidate at the University of Edinburgh. His thesis is a study of the work of Louis MacNeice and his influence on contemporary Northern Irish and Scottish poets. Dave is currently working on his first collection of poems, and writes reviews of new poetry releases at http://davepoems.wordpress.com.

BOB COLLINS was Chief Commissioner of the Equality Commission for Northern Ireland between August 2005 and January 2012, and is a former Director-General of RTÉ. He has served as a member of the Boards of the National Concert Hall, the National Library of Ireland and of the Ulster Orchestra Society. He was a member of Comhairle Theilifís na Gaeilge and is Chair of the Broadcasting Authority of Ireland.

DIANE FAHEY is the author of twelve poetry collections, most recently *The Wing Collection: New & Selected Poems* (Puncher & Wattmann, 2011) and *The Stone Garden: Poems from Clare* (Clouds of Magellan, 2013). She has received many literary grants and awards for her poetry, and was selected for Australian Poetry's 2013 International Poetry Tour of Ireland. Diane has been awarded residencies at Hawthornden International Writers' Centre, and the Tyrone Guthrie Centre, and been writer in residence at Ormond College, Melbourne, and the University of Adelaide.

ALAN GILLIS teaches at Edinburgh University. His fourth collection of poetry is due to be published in late 2014.

EAMONN HUGHES is a senior lecturer in the School of English at Queen's University, Belfast and Assistant Director of the Institute of Irish Studies. He is a regular contributor to Irish cultural publications and broadcasts regularly on arts and culture on BBCNI. His short history of Irish literature was broadcast by BBCNI in 50 episodes from April to June 2009. He is currently writing a literary history of Belfast.

FRED JOHNSTON is the author of several novels and two collections of short stories. His translation of the work of Breton poet Colette Wittorski is published by Lapwing Press, Belfast, and his ninth collection of poetry, *Alligator Days*, was published earlier this year. He lives in Galway, where he is director of the Western Writers' Centre - Ionad Scríbhneoirí Chaitlín Maude.

[*128*]

EDNA LONGLEY is Professor Emerita in the school of English, Queen's University, Belfast. Her most recent publication is *Yeats and Modern Poetry* (Cambridge University Press, 2013).

DONAL MAHONEY has had poetry and fiction published in *The Galway Review, Revival, The Stony Thursday Book, The Linnet's Wings, ROPES* and other publications in North America, Europe, Asia and Africa. He has been nominated for Best of the Net and Pushcart prizes. Some of his earliest work can be found at http://booksonblog12.blogspot.com

JOHN MCAULIFFE's third book, *Of All Places* (Gallery, 2011) was a PBS Recommendation. He teaches poetry at the University of Manchester's Centre for New Writing and writes a monthly poetry column for the Irish Times.

GAIL MCCONNELL is a lecturer in English at Queen's University. Her monograph, *Northern Irish Poetry and Theology,* will be published by Palgrave in 2014.

KATHLEEN MCCRACKEN is the author of seven collections of poetry including *Blue Light, Bay and College, Mooncalves* and *Tattoo Land,* and her poems have been published in *The Malahat Review, Poetry Canada Review, Exile Quarterly, Poetry Ireland, New Orleans Review, the SHOp, Revival* and *Abridged.* She is currently Lecturer in English Literature and Creative Writing at the University of Ulster.

BRIDGET MEEDS' long poem 'Light' was published in the trio volume *Wild Workshop* (Faber and Faber, UK, 1997) and in *American Poetry Review* in 1998. She has published two full collections of poetry: *Tuning the Beam* (2000) and *Audience* (2007), and has had poems and essays appear in a number of magazines. She has an M.A. from Lancaster University's Poets House and a B.A. from Ithaca College. She is the co-founder and chair of Ithaca City of Asylum, which host dissident writers in Ithaca, NY.

FRED POLLACK is the author of two book-length narrative poems, *The Adventure* and *Happiness,* both published by Story Line Press, and has had other poems in print and online journals. Fred is adjunct professor creative writing George Washington University.

CAROL RUMENS was formerly Writer-in-Residence at Queen's University, Belfast and is now Lecturer in Creative Writing at the University of Wales, Bangor. Her most recent collection of poems is *De Chirico's Threads* (Seren, 2010).

STEPHEN SEXTON lives in Belfast where he is studying for a PhD in Creative Writing at the Seamus Heaney Centre for Poetry.

CONNIE VOISINE is an associate professor of English at New Mexico State University Her collection *Cathedral of the North* won the AWP Award for Poetry and her second collecton, *Rare High Meadow of Which I Might Dream* was published by University of Chicago Press in 2008. She was recently a Fulbright Scholar at Queen's University Belfast.

DAVID WHEATLEY is the author of *The Reed Bunting Unseen: A Camouflage Garden for Ian Hamilton Finlay* (Wild Honey Press).

JOHN WHEWAY's poems have appeared in *New Measure, Stand, Magma, The Warwick Review, Poetry Review*; his work is also in the anthologies *Bliss* and *Octopus* from Templar, and *The Echoing Gallery* from Redcliffe Press. His chapbook *The Green Table of Infinity* was published by Anvil Press Poetry, and a novella, *Poborden* was included in *Introduction 3* from Faber and Faber. He is a psychotherapist and has an MA in Creative Writing from Bath Spa.